The Identity ATM

Eric Bryan

Montaut Publishing, LLC.

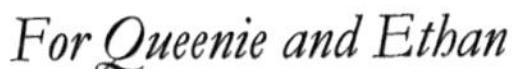

For Queenie and Ethan

Table Of Contents

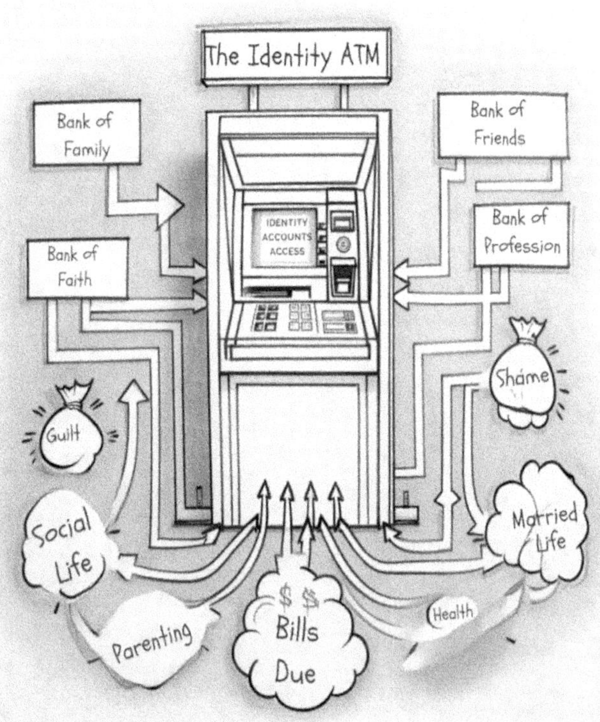

The Identity ATM
Bank of Family
Bank of Friends
Bank of Faith
Bank of Profession
IDENTITY ACCOUNTS ACCESS
Guilt
Shame
Social Life
Married Life
Parenting
$ $ Bills Due
Health

Introduction

In the heart of bustling New York City, Gregory, a mid-40s-year-old investment banker, went about his daily life meticulously managing financial transactions, helping businesses grow, and ensuring all his clients' investments yielded the highest returns. He wore tailored suits, his shoes always polished, and he had an air of certainty that, over the years, had become his trademark. His clients valued his expertise and dedication. But for all his financial acumen, Gregory had yet to realize that life's most valuable transactions took place outside the marbled floors of the bank.

One evening, after an unusually long day at work, Gregory walked to his favorite cafe, aiming to grab a cup of coffee and some solitude. He sat at a corner table, lost in his thoughts when he noticed an older gentleman, probably in his late seventies, staring intently at him from across the room. The older man's piercing blue eyes seemed to be taking an inventory of Gregory's soul. Unsettled but intrigued, Gregory decided to approach him. "Is there something I can help you with, sir?" he asked, trying to sound as polite as possible.

The older man smiled gently. "I've been observing you," he began, "and I see my younger self in you. Always in a hurry, always calculating. But tell me, have you ever considered that every interaction, every moment and relationship, is also a transaction toward your transformation?"

Gregory, taken aback, blinked a few times before responding, "I'm not sure I follow."

The man continued, "I spent decades where you are now. Maybe not with the same style or at the same bank, but the same, if you understand what I'm saying. In every moment of our lives, every encounter we have with another soul, we're making deposits or withdrawals. It's joy, shame, guilt, love. These are the real ones."

Over the next few weeks, Gregory and the older man, Elias, met several times. With each meeting, Elias shared more about his own life, his regrets, and the lessons he'd learned. He spoke of times when he'd made meaningful emotional deposits into people's lives, moments of compassion and genuine connection. He also shared painful memories of withdrawals and times when he'd acted out of ego, anger, or impatience.

Gregory began to see his own interactions differently over time. He recalled how he'd hastily brushed off a colleague's attempt at conversation, making a withdrawal. Or when he'd failed to appreciate his team's efforts, missing out on an opportunity to make a deposit. The toll of missed opportunities and unobserved emotional transactions began to bear on him.

Introduction

One evening, as they sat in their familiar booth and routine, Elias handed Gregory a worn-out journal. "This," Elias began, "was my tool for change. Every day, I'd jot down the deposits I made and the withdrawals that occurred. Not to judge myself, but to become more aware. It doesn't have to be a journal for you but find something that helps you process and find value in life's transactions."

Following Elias's advice, Gregory started by maintaining a journal. With every entry, he became more attuned to his emotional transactions. He started to see the patterns in the times of day when he was more likely to be impatient or interactions that triggered feelings of inadequacy or shame.

As the months went by, journaling changed Gregory's perspective on life. He began to see himself not just as an investment banker but as a man engaged in the continuous process of exchange. He worked on making more deposits, offering compliments freely, exuberantly excelling as a listening ear, expressing gratitude, and being more present in every interaction.

The ripple effect of this change was immense. Gregory's relationships flourished. Colleagues began to approach him more, clients appreciated his newfound empathy, and even the barista at his favorite cafe noted the change. "You seem lighter," she remarked one day.

The most revelatory change, however, was internal. With each positive transaction, Gregory felt a shift in his identity. He felt more in tune with his emotions and more genuine in his expressions. The masks of pride, pretense, and impatience he'd worn for years began to fall away, revealing a more authentic, compassionate, and connected man.

The tale of Gregory is not just the story of one man's awakening to life's genuine transactions. It's a universal reminder that our interactions, big or small, shape our identity, our relationships, and, ultimately, our legacy. Every transaction matters. And in the end, the wealthiest life is filled with meaningful deposits of love and genuine connection.

Our identity amalgamates our beliefs, experiences, values, and self-perceptions. It is the expression of who you are or believe yourself to be integrated into the presence of emotions like guilt and shame, which can influence how we present ourselves.

Guilt, often stemming from our actions or perceived failures concerning our personal or societal standards, can act as a moral compass. It signals a discrepancy between our actions and our values. When guilt becomes a dominant factor in our identity, it can manifest in various ways. We might become overly apologetic, constantly seeking validation or reassurance. Some might also develop a heightened sense of responsibility, striving to make amends or avoid situations where they might "fail" again. While guilt can lead to positive change and personal growth when addressed constructively, unchecked guilt can result in a constant feeling of unworthiness or perpetually on edge as it becomes the truth we live by.

Shame, on the other hand, pushes deeper. It's not just about feeling bad for something we did; it's feeling wrong about who we are. Shame makes us question our inherent worthiness. When shame colors our identity, it can also drive a profound sense of inadequacy. This feeling often results in individuals hiding aspects of themselves, fearing judgment or rejection. They might construct walls, revealing only those parts deemed "acceptable" or "normal" by societal standards. Over time, this ushers in a fragmented self, where the public persona starkly contrasts with the inner self. Shame can also drive self-isolating behaviors, as individuals might feel they don't "belong" or are fundamentally flawed.

In both emotional responses, the weight of guilt and shame can stifle genuine self-expression. Instead of captivated lives aligned with our authentic selves, we might find ourselves trapped in cycles of appeasement, avoidance, or even self-punishment, but not truth. Through introspection, therapy, or open conversations, individuals can disentangle their identity from these limiting emotions, paving the way for a more authentic, compassionate, and self-affirming expression of self.

When we look at an ATM (Automated Teller Machine), it's easy to focus solely on its physical presence: the machine where we can directly access our funds. However, behind this standalone device lies a network of systems, databases, and infrastructures that belong to a bank. This connection between the ATM and its bank is complete and seamless, even if it's not immediately visible to us. We interact with ATMs, aware but perhaps not fully conscious, that our bank previously ensured there are funds in the machine.

Drawing a parallel to our lives, just as an ATM is connected to a bank, individuals are deeply connected to their foundational pillars: faith, family, and context. A person's context typically encompasses their work and social lives, considering the time spent in each of them. These foundational elements are often your emotional bank, influencing your decisions, shaping your identity, and guiding your values, even if you aren't always consciously aware of their presence. In fact, most are surprised to learn how much it impacts them without their knowing entirely.

Banks and Personal Foundations

The Bank of Faith

Much like the secure databases of a bank that guarantee the correct transaction and balance accuracy, faith acts as a fast and foundational database for many. It advertises as a system of beliefs, values, and guidelines. Faith makes available a personal belief system that provides direction, solace, and meaning even for those who might not subscribe to a particular religion. The value of our identity shapes how we spend it.

Faith grants a sacred space to process our emotions against higher values. Our emotions and beliefs often represent the most significant tension in our lives. This is experienced when we fight for what we want and the unlimited ways we sense *life* isn't working in that favor. Faith is deposited into our well-being. In its many forms, religion is a bedrock of support and assurance for countless individuals worldwide. For many, faith proffers a sanctuary of hope and optimism, a milieu to face adversity and uncertainty. By believing in something greater than oneself, whether it's a higher power, the tenets of a religious doctrine, or the essential good in humanity, individuals often find inner strength and resilience they might not have realized they possessed. This belief system can act as a buffer against life's harsh realities and curveballs, allowing individuals to traverse difficult situations with a sense of purpose when life pulls them into the indebtedness of a momentary problem. The bank of faith is unique when compared to the others, when there is a disparity between our feelings and our beliefs, creating a dynamic as if they were headbutting each other.

But overall, faith is healthy and introduces a sense of community and belongingness our identity needs. Humans naturally seek validation; faith-based communities often put forth these essential elements. Faith communities have also scientifically been proven to improve the emotional richness of life, such as decreasing anxiety, depression, and suicidal behavior – all responses to how we process guilt and shame. Being part of such a community harbors feelings of acceptance, love, and mutual support. These positive social interactions and bonds contribute to mental and emotional well-being. The feeling that one is part of something larger and that there are like-minded individuals who share the same beliefs can be deeply comforting, reducing feelings of loneliness or isolation.

Lastly, faith instills a moral and ethical framework that guides individuals daily. This ethical grounding often promotes compassion, forgiveness, and selflessness. By striving to live according to these principles, individuals often experience a sense of fulfillment and meaning in their actions and decisions. Furthermore, faith-based practices, such as meditation and prayer, can be therapeutic. Moments of solace, introspection, and connection with one's inner self correspond with depositing immeasurable value into one's well-being.

The Bank of Family

The bank's infrastructure, which supports the smooth functioning of every ATM, can be likened to our families. They may offer support and guidance and clearly explain when you shouldn't be buying items outside your means. From our early years, family imprints on us certain traditions, values, and beliefs that form the backbone of our identity.

Our family participates in shaping our identity and self-worth. Like an ATM's relationship with its bank, our interactions with family members involve deposits that enrich our sense of self and withdrawals that might deplete it, all requiring detection of the nuances of these transactions.

Deposits from family include unconditional love, affirmations, support during setbacks, and serving as role models. Being accepted, especially during formative years, is pivotal in building self-worth. Words of encouragement, praise, and acknowledgment for their role (parent to child and child to parent as you age) make deposits. Hearing a parent, sibling, or relative express pride in our achievements or appreciating our character traits fortifies our self-esteem. When we face setbacks or failures, the supportive embrace of the family can act as a buffer, verifying that our self-worth isn't drastically affected. Family members who embody values, skills, or attributes we admire can be role models. Their presence and example positively add to our self-worth, showing us what's attainable.

What is essential with the bank of family is how self-worth funds are transferred. Managing open communication, external affirmations, and establishing healthy boundaries help us confirm when transactions occur. This mitigates the impact of all potential withdrawals and builds interest upon the deposit. It simply comes down to curiosity and caring with the ability to communicate it.

The Bank of Context

An individual's immediate environment or context is like the geographical location of an ATM. Just as an ATM's utility and function might slightly vary based on its site (a mall, airport, or remote village), our experiences, choices, and perspectives are influenced by the context we find ourselves in, be it urban or rural, affluent or struggling, peaceful or turbulent.

Our life context, the environment we live in, the experiences we undergo, the adversities we face, and even the daily routines we adopt influences the shaping of our emotional landscape. Our emotions, sculpted from our experiences, reach the depth and richness of our identity's expression.

The cultural environment we're exposed to and raised in influences our emotional palette. For instance, some cultures prioritize communal values, advocating emotions related to empathy, solidarity, and shared joy. In contrast, others might emphasize individual achievements, intensifying the focus on emotions like pride or self-satisfaction. Urban and rural settings introduce different life experiences. City life might expose one to feelings related to ambition, competition, or isolation. In contrast, rural settings might facilitate a deep connection to nature, simplicity, and community bonding.

The context of our personal experiences, such as triumphs and failures, brings emotions like joy, pride, and fulfillment. Losses, while initially bringing disappointment or sadness, can, over time, add layers of resilience, determination, and a more profound discovery of oneself. Relationships, from familial bonds to friendships and romantic relationships, extend over our emotional spectrum. Love, trust, betrayal, jealousy, companionship from each relationship colors new shades to our emotional canvas.

Other contexts, such as our socioeconomic status and one of the most considerable contexts for adults, our jobs, make deposits and withdrawals. Affluence and financial comfort grant experiences of luxury, leisure, and a broadened worldview. But it might also introduce emotions related to the fear of loss or the pressure to maintain a particular lifestyle.

Economic hurdles too high can attract feelings of despair, insecurity, or constant stress. But they can also instill resilience, grit, gratitude for the little things, and a strong sense of community and shared struggles.

Our work and jobs often serve as a central pillar in defining our life context. They award economic sustenance and a sense of purpose, identity, and belonging. The nature of our job, role within an organization, work culture, and relationships with colleagues all influence our daily experiences and self-perception. For many, a job is desired to be more than just a means to earn; it reflects their passions, skills, and longings for a better society. However, this centrality also means that battles at work, be it conflicts, dissatisfaction, or instability, can profoundly impact our well-being, self-esteem, and overall life context. The significance of our work life underscores seeking alignment between our job roles and our personal values, aspirations, and emotional needs.

So be careful who you bank with. Life's transactions can be tough, extremely tough. But they can be just as equally rewarding. Values, morals, and ethics are formed in the difficulties we face. People are shaped in these regards by enduring tough moments and learning what worked for them in those moments. Events such as divorce, failing an exam, suicide, or grief formulate beliefs within us more than going to an amusement park or taking a cruise vacation does.

It is worth revealing that, unfortunately, sometimes engaging with faith and family makes more withdrawals than deposits into our well-being. Families may well encapsulate the foundational support for emotional, mental, and sometimes even physical well-being. They can, in specific contexts, become sources of distress. Dysfunctional family dynamics, which may include overbearing expectations, feeble comparisons, emotional manipulation, or even abuse, formulate chronic stress, self-doubt, and mental illnesses. Family members' criticisms or dismissive attitudes, especially when repeated over time, can erode an individual's self-worth, making them vulnerable to anxiety, depression, and feelings of isolation. Therefore, business leaders and managers are encouraged to welcome their new employees to the team, not the family, as the association with family may create barriers to that connection.

When someone overwhelmingly must receive constructive criticism, comparison, overbearing expectations, neglect, or indifference, especially without guidance or support, it withdraws from our self-worth. Phrases like "You'll never amount to anything" or "Why can't you be like …?" can erode one's confidence. These tend to create feelings of inadequacy.

In like manner, faith, often seen as a source of solace and guidance, can sometimes become a double-edged sword. Dogmatic beliefs or rigid religious interpretations can proliferate guilt, fear, or shame, especially if individuals don't meet their faith standards. Furthermore, faith communities can sometimes ostracize or stigmatize members who question, doubt, or live outside prescribed norms, enticing them to alienation and spiritual distress. Similarly, our broader context, including societal norms, peer groups, and community expectations, can exert immense pressure. Living in environments that are discriminatory, intolerant, or unsupportive can create a perpetual state of alertness and distress, severely impacting mental well-being and overall life satisfaction. This book will also shift our view of life transactions and transitions. We experience various phases of growth, from the innocence and wonder of childhood to the rebelliousness of teenage years and the introspection of middle age; each life phase is unique in its emotional experiences. Major life events, like marriage, parenthood, or career changes, introduce a whirlwind of emotions, from joy and anticipation to anxiety and doubt. Personal and professional dilemmas dive immensely into our emotional depth, amplifying the physical impact of stress on the body. These experiences teach us resilience, patience, and the value of hope and perseverance.

Culture is akin to the bank's operating system that manages various ATMs. Each bank may have its unique software, protocols, and procedures. Similarly, every culture has its customs, traditions, and norms. Even as we operate as individuals (like standalone ATMs), our actions, thoughts, and beliefs often align with the cultural "software" ingrained in us.

Our emotional richness is a direct resemblance to our life context. Every experience, whether positive or negative, adds depth to our emotional cognizance. By embracing our unique life context, we experience a broad spectrum of emotions and a more fulfilled life. Uncovering this emotional richness also fosters empathy as we establish how our context has shaped ourselves and how the contexts of others have similarly influenced their emotional landscapes.

An ATM is a mere access point to a much more extensive banking system. Our Identity ATM manifests an expression based upon knowing how our identity banks deliver insights, thus value, into our behaviors and decisions, emphasizing the interplay of various forces in shaping our lives.

The Role of the Identity ATM

Becoming conscious of your Identity ATM isn't just an exercise in self-awareness; it's a journey towards self-transformation. This book aims to be a guide, helping readers handle the intricacies of their life transactions. Through subsequent chapters, we will dive deeper into deposits, withdrawals, many external influences, and strategies for achieving a positive balance that lead to connecting with your true self.

In an age where mental health is rightfully gaining prominence, mastering the Identity ATM is not just beneficial, it's essential. As readers embark on this introspective journey, they'll be equipped with the tools better vetting options, regardless of life's trials.

To close this introductory chapter, consider this: every interaction, decision, and experience is an opportunity for transformation. By being mindful of them, we can achieve a more prosperous, fulfilling, expressive life. The goal isn't merely to avoid negative balances but to cultivate a wealth of favorable emotional currency, safeguarding resilience, joy, and fulfillment in our daily lives. Each chapter will begin with the chapter concept and a strategy towards enrichment and will end with questions to engage with the material presented.

The Identity ATM

Chapter Concept: Our identity is likened to an ATM, with access to accounts of self-esteem and confidence, our psyche's version of savings and checking accounts.

Chapter Strategy for Enrichment: Explore how our internal processes become external expressions of who we are, guiding how transactions become transformation.

The foundation of *The Identity ATM* is a result of thousands of one-on-one, marriage and family, professional, and organizational counseling sessions over the past thirty years. The mental processing framework that the Identity ATM presents has been the catalyst for helping people process the events in their life, more times than not, all happening at the same time. It is very common to be dealt bad news while trying to handle other unfortunate events. For example, being fired from a job during your ongoing divorce or losing a friend to suicide while your kids are failing in school. Life is happening all around us and within us simultaneously. The Identity ATM is a way to explore and contextualize the manner in which we process these events we know are impacting us but sometimes can't fully articulate how or why.

In the banking system of our mind, there lies an ATM. This is the Identity ATM. Unlike conventional ATMs, which dispense cash, this machine manages the currencies of who we are and how we express ourselves: self-worth, confidence, guilt, shame, joy, and despair. To benefit from the transactions in life, it is essential to have a positive balance of mental and emotional currency to spend.

In the heart of our internal being, where thoughts collide, and emotions flow, often countering our values and principles, the Identity ATM bolted down to our core stands ready to dispense funds. Every day, whether we're conscious of it or not, we make transactions at this ATM. The deposits and withdrawals determine our emotional solvency and shape our interactions with the world. Picture this: walking into a room filled with strangers. Does the balance in your Identity ATM allow you to approach them confidently? Or does a deficit make you retreat, mired in self-doubt? Do you have joy and contentment when others receive great news, or do you circle the conversation back to why good things don't happen to you?

At a fundamental level, this concept isn't new. Philosophers, psychologists, and life coaches have long discussed the internal value system determining our self-worth. However, the analogy of the Identity ATM brings a modern, relatable perspective to an age-old dilemma. With this metaphor, we can better grasp the complexities of our mental and emotional transactions depending on where our identity banks.

As mentioned, we have banks that our psyche is connected to that either provide us with funds deposited or make us aware of how life makes withdrawals. Influences from our parents, teachers, peers, and society at large from our early beginnings create initial deposits and withdrawals. A child praised for their efforts might receive a significant guarantee in their self-worth account. Conversely, a child ridiculed may face a substantial withdrawal and be left with a receipt of shame, like an adult rejected at an ATM due to insufficient funds available. These early transactions set the tone for future interactions, and over time, patterns emerge.

As we grow, our experiences become multifaceted. The black-and-white nature of childhood experiences starts to blend into a spectrum of grays. The Identity ATM's balance becomes more fluid, reflecting the heart of our life experiences. A high school athlete might enjoy a surge in confidence with every win but might also grapple with shame if their academic grades don't meet a parent's expectations. Many celebrities have displayed a struggle between being confident in their abilities, extremely competent even, but still overwhelmed with shame, some to the point of suicide. It is my belief you are more than one aspect of your behavior. You are more than your heritage, your sexuality, your political affiliation, etc.

Balancing Acts and Emotional Overdrafts

Maintaining a robust balance and steady stream of revenue is no easy task. Life may present itself as an enemy after our mental and emotional reserves. Relationship issues, work environment, societal expectations, and personal aspirations can lead to transactions with the different accounts we access at our Identity ATM. Just like a financial ATM, there are times when we might face an emotional overdraft. Overdrawing from our self-worth can manifest in numerous ways: feelings of inadequacy, anxiety, or shame. But unlike banks, which charge a fee for financial overdrafts, the costs of emotional overdrafts are far more reaching, affecting our mental health, relationships, and overall well-being. More on this in chapter four, where the discussion on identity theft occurs.

Emotional and mental overdrafts, much like their financial counterparts, may lead to deficits where the individual has no reserves to draw upon. Suicide and suicidal ideations are mental states encapsulating all of the individual's thoughts and feelings without a healthy manner to process them. The toll of overdraft is immense, multiplying stress, anxiety, and debt due to psychological, physiological, and many more emotional factors. At this point, it is extremely difficult to remain objective towards a different version of the immediate future that doesn't include death.

When you consider the Identity ATM's role in general, it is easier to objectively comprehend how the depleted levels of self-esteem and confidence result in increased levels of shame and the feeling of bankruptcy, lying to your identity, and longing to close your account for good. Mental health professionals can provide support when experiencing those difficulties to help you in times of need. The metaphor of emotional and mental overdraft to financial depletion is a powerful one that helps to conceptualize the impact of prolonged stress. Understanding this can encourage empathy for those in this perilous state and be a call to action to provide the necessary resources for deposits to reoccur.

Not every situation of overdraft will result in contemplating suicide, but it is very draining. Amid that moment, even little deposits into your emotional and mental well-being bring awareness of one's cost of living.

Awareness to insight to action.

The processes involved with the Identity ATM are about the journey from self-awareness to insight and eventually to action. This lies at the heart of personal growth and development. This progression is prominent for individual well-being and effective interpersonal relationships with the broader community. Self-awareness is the starting point for uncovering our emotions, strengths, weaknesses, thoughts, and motivations. This doesn't simply mean endorsing these facets on a surface level but delving deep into them, questioning their origins and impact on our actions and reactions.

By being self-aware, we gain the necessary insights as to why we feel a certain way in particular situations or why specific triggers evoke thoughts and, eventually, intense emotions. It also means pointing out our patterns, behaviors, ideas, and emotions that recur in various circumstances. For instance, our irritability escalates when we're stressed or sleep deprived. This mitigates those feelings before they negatively impact our relationships or decision-making. Thus, the first step in mastering our Identity ATM is awareness. Just as one might regularly check their bank balance to manage their finances, being attuned to our emotional balance is the start to managing our thoughts, feelings, and expressions.

Interpreting when we're low on confidence or guilt is consuming our reserves takes corrective actions. One of the most challenging aspects is distinguishing between genuine withdrawals, based on introspection, and imposed withdrawals, dictated by external factors such as unrealistic expectations. The latter often sways to unnecessary emotional expenditures, draining our reserves and leaving us feeling hollow.

While self-awareness provides a foundation, insight is the bridge that connects thought to actionable change. Insight means concluding the patterns we observe in ourselves. It's about connecting seemingly unrelated events, feelings, or behaviors. For example, a person might detect through self-awareness that they often feel anxious before team meetings. Delving into this emotion might promote insight that this anxiety stems from a fear of public speaking, rooted in a childhood experience of being mocked while speaking in front of a class. Here, the insight is citing deep-seated fear and its origin, not merely the surface-level anxiety before meetings. Insight also involves conceding both positive and negative patterns. Positive patterns reinforce them. For instance, one who thrives in collaborative settings can guide future work or group activity decisions.

You're now equipped for action with the foundation of self-awareness and the bridge of insight. In this context, action is doing something that aligns with our true self, expressing our thought patterns. The action taken becomes the expression of our identity. Using the previous example, if one has insight into their fear of public speaking, the action might involve joining a public speaking course or seeking opportunities to practice in a safe environment. Conversely, if someone identifies a strength in collaborative settings, the action might involve seeking out team projects or considering career paths prioritizing teamwork.

Moreover, the action isn't a one-time event. It's a continuous process of refining and redefining behaviors, reactions, and decisions based on the evolving nature. As our self-awareness grows and our insights gain clarity, our actions will shift, commencing a cycle of continuous personal growth.

Identity Transactions: Deposits, Withdrawals, and the Balance of Life Events

Drawing on the ATM metaphor, just as financial transactions dictate the balance of our bank accounts, our life events make deposits and withdrawals of our identity, affecting our emotional and mental processing balance.

Life events that serve as deposits usually bolster our self-esteem and confidence accounts. These deposits can come from achievements, both personal and professional milestones, completing a degree program, earning a promotion, receiving positive affirmations, learning and experiencing new things, and being part of a vigorous relationship. These positive reinforcements boost our sense of belonging and affirm validation from our community and context. They deposit value, self-worth, self-esteem, confidence, forgiveness, and mercy.

Conversely, certain life events can attempt to commit identity theft. These might include failures or setbacks. Whether it's a project that didn't pan out, a job loss, or personal disappointments, these events can temporarily diminish our self-worth or confidence. Negative or continuous criticism or derogatory remarks can chip away at our self-esteem, especially when not constructive. Traumatic events or prolonged periods of stress and anxiety set a trend that to cope; one must consistently make substantial withdrawals from their well-being. The loss of a loved one, the end of a relationship, or the loss of a dream can deeply impact our sense of self.

The Identity ATM

Maintaining a Positive Balance

A consistent income affirms our identity remains whole and sustained. Replenishment after withdrawals, just as we might deposit money after an expense, we should seek activities or support systems that restore our emotional well-being after an adverse life event. As discussed in the introduction, our Identity ATM, where we get our funds, is linked to our bank. The connections to our banks may be through therapy, practicing our faith or religion, leaning on loved ones, being trained and developed in our jobs, participating in healing practices like meditation or journaling, and other endless ways to receive funds of confidence, self-esteem, and growth.

Regular monitoring, just as one regularly checks their bank balance, and frequent self-examination shows we're aware of our emotional state, helping us address potential deficits. Investing wisely, in financial terms, yields long-term benefits. Similarly, investing time in nurturing relationships, continuous learning, and self-care sustains long-term deposits into our identity. Our identity is constantly in flux, influenced by life events and transactions we experience. By marking these as deposits and withdrawals, we can actively maintain a positive balance and authenticate a robust and resilient sense of self throughout life's ups and downs. This diligence, sometimes the sheer grit and gumption, is what separates you from believing the lies you sometimes tell yourself. The Identity ATM operates as that access point to conduct this monitoring.

Questions for Reflection:

1. How would you describe yourself in three words?
2. What are some of your core values and beliefs?
3. Can you identify a recent event that made you feel very emotional and why it affected you?
4. How do you usually react when faced with conflict or criticism?
5. Can you recall a recent mistake and what you learned from it?
6. Are there certain situations or triggers that consistently evoke strong emotions in you?
7. When was the last time you took a moment for self-analysis?
8. How do you usually process your feelings and experiences?
9. How do your surroundings and those around you influence your thoughts and behaviors?

Identity Deposits: Building Self-Worth and Confidence

Chapter Concept: Guilt arises from our actions, while shame is linked to our sense of self-worth.

Chapter Strategy for Enrichment: Identify how prolonged guilt or shame can erode our self-esteem and confidence.

With every achievement, validation, and positive affirmation, we are making deposits into our Identity ATM accounts of self-esteem and confidence. Like financial savings, these deposits give us emotional resilience and buffer against life in emergencies and upcoming lifestyle changes. In banking, a deposit signifies growth, security, and prosperity. Emotional deposits are paramount for espousing self-worth and confidence in our Identity ATM. These deposits are affirmations, validations, and experiences that fortify our sense of self. They are emotional anchors, grounding us during storms of doubt and uncertainty. It is a widely held belief to be financially secure, one should have a minimum of six months of savings available in case 'life happens' and other needs arise requiring emergency funds. How many, though, are living paycheck to paycheck? Similarly, how are you doing with emotional or mental wealth? Do you have enough to spend if there is a hefty transaction, such as losing a job, moving to a new country, or going through a divorce?

The Fabric of Self-Worth

Self-worth is a deeply entrenched belief about our inherent value. It's not just about what we can do or have achieved; it's about who we are at our core. While external achievements can boost our self-worth, their true essence lies in internal acceptance. Seeing our worth irrespective of external validations is the cornerstone of genuine self-esteem. The methods discussed in this chapter to build self-worth come from discussing confidence, authenticity, connections, and navigating change in our lives. Grieving also affects us, more than most expect, in our ability to tap into our self-worth.

Every time we acknowledge our inherent value, there is a deposit into our Identity ATM. These deposits stem from various sources mentioned in Chapter One. Meeting personal goals, whether fitness milestones, academic accomplishments, or career advancements, bolsters our sense of capability.

Words have power. When someone appreciates our efforts or our qualities, it reinforces our awareness. Facing adversity head-on and emerging stronger is a testament to our resilience, adding to our identity reserves.

While self-worth lies deep within, confidence is its outward manifestation or expression of our identity. It's a currency we use to interact with the world. Confidence takes analyzed risks, asserting ourselves, and standing firm in our beliefs. It's the fuel that drives our actions and shapes our interactions. Typically, the more someone participates in their work, the more confident they become doing that work. Skill mastery and becoming proficient in a particular skill reinforces our belief in our abilities. This could be mastering a musical instrument, excelling in a sport, or honing a craft. Building meaningful relationships via social interactions and connecting with others adds layers to our confidence. Every positive social interaction can serve as a deposit, no matter how small. One central area of adding confidence to our bank account is how well we embrace ambiguity in our lives. Being genuine to oneself and accepted for it is a powerful confidence booster when there are uncertain seasons to work through. It reinforces the idea that we are enough as we are.

However, the danger to confidence is being too confident, crossing over into arrogance. Imagine someone owning and driving a Ferrari or Lamborghini but they live on a dirt road in a poor town. Confidence needs the proper context and freedom, or you may come across as needy, cocky, and perhaps even insecure.

Embracing authenticity is the preferred method for generating emotional wealth. Continuous learning, mindfulness and analysis, constructive feedback, and setting healthy boundaries mean we look through the correct lens of life and learn what is true about our life and what isn't. Adopting this mindset and being open to learning displays frequent deposits that have been made. Every new piece of knowledge or skill acquired adds to our emotional wealth. Regular introspection helps in comprehending our strengths and efforts. Setting aside time for inner probing can yield rich emotional dividends. Opening up to trusted individuals who provide honest, constructive feedback is an invaluable asset. Such interactions pledge insights into areas of improvement, as well as affirmations of our strengths to ensure the deposits aren't depleted by external negativity and debilitating factors.

Authenticity is found at the heart of genuine confidence. Embracing sincerity means aligning and being grounded with one's true self, values, beliefs, and experiences. It's about shedding pretenses, embracing vulnerabilities, and showcasing an unfiltered version of oneself to the world. This trustworthy validity is rooted in self-awareness. We establish a strong internal foundation by piecing together our feelings, strengths, weaknesses, desires, and values. This foundation stipulates that our actions and reactions are consistent and authentic to who we are, showcasing a natural confidence that isn't easily shaken by external opinions or situations. When there's a misalignment between our actions and our true selves, it creates cognitive dissonance. This is a state of mental discomfort. Living credibly reduces this dissonance, resulting in a sense of harmony within oneself, further enhancing self-assuredness.

Additionally, it fosters trust. People learn to trust our words and actions when we consistently present our genuine selves. This external validation, while not the primary goal of an unfeigned identity, can further boost our confidence.

Accepting our vulnerabilities, registering in our minds that it's okay not to be perfect, and appreciating that our vulnerabilities don't define our worth frees us from the stress of unrealistic expectations. Over time, this acceptance produces resilience and a more robust sense of self-worth. Transparency helps differentiate between constructive criticism and baseless judgment. This clarity empowers them to negotiate objections with grace and self-assurance. This highlights the need to protect genuine relationships, culminating with even deeper, more meaningful relationships with self and others. When we're honest, we attract individuals who resonate with our true selves. These uncontrived relationships, built on mutual respect, can serve as a supportive foundation, enhancing our confidence in social scenarios.

As confidence builds, the individual shifts away from flawed thinking and emotional expressions. Paired with a genuine internalization of the transactions, this presides over goals and actions that mirror one's inner values and passions. Living with purpose and intention not only brings fulfillment but also instills a sense of confidence in our path and decisions. Authenticity is a humble confidence. It's a continuous journey of self-discovery, acceptance, and growth. By embracing our true selves, we bolster a deep sense of self-worth and self-assuredness and honestly cater to our relationships and experiences with the world around us. Personal fulfillment becomes immeasurable despite the path to get there being fraught with vulnerabilities.

We are social beings, and our interactions contribute to our emotional well-being. Connecting with support groups, be it family, friends, or interest groups, establishes routine deposits in our Identity ATM. Connections award validation; being part of a group where our feelings, experiences, and beliefs are validated fortifies our self-worth. They also offer shared experiences. Engaging in group activities or shared experiences builds collective confidence, boosting individual confidence. And they also tender accountability. When we commit to goals or actions with an intentional community, collective accountability can serve as motivation and a sense of achievement when dreams are realized.

Connections are intrinsic to human nature. From our earliest moments as infants seeking the comfort of a caregiver's touch to our later years when bonds with friends and family become even more vital, the human journey is characterized by connections and one's pursuit of connections, keeping in mind not all connections are created equal. Healthy connections grounded in mutual respect and trust are essential for physical, emotional, and psychological well-being. From a biological standpoint, humans are wired for connection. Our brains release oxytocin, often called the 'bonding' hormone, during close human interaction, such as hugging or deep conversation. This hormone doesn't merely induce feelings of warmth and affection; it also has many physiological benefits. It can reduce stress hormones, lower blood pressure, and boost immune system function. Moreover, studies have shown that social isolation or consistently negative social interactions directly impact a host of issues, including increased risk of cardiovascular diseases, lowered immune response, and even premature mortality.

Our connections introduce us to diverse perspectives, cultures, beliefs, and experiences. They expand our horizons, making us more tolerant, empathetic, and knowledgeable. Whether it's being enlightened by a new culture through a friend, exploring a new hobby introduced by a family member, or challenging our beliefs through discussions, flourishing connections make us more rounded individuals.

Radiant connections also stimulate a sense of responsibility and accountability. They instill in us values of honesty, integrity, and commitment. Knowing that our actions affect our loved ones makes us more conscious of our decisions and behaviors. These connections are not just beneficial; they're essential. They shape our experiences, mold our personalities, and dictate our happiness levels. While the digital age has exponentially increased our connectivity, the quality of these connections matters more than quantity. Flourishing relations should be a conscious endeavor, for they are the bedrock of a fulfilled, healthy, and meaningful life.

One well-known fact about life is change is the only constant. Healthy connections play a pivotal role as we chart a course through life's various transitions — from school to university, from singlehood to partnership, and from one career to another. They share advice, their experiences, emotional support, and resources. What is taking place beneath the surface in these changes is grieving. Grief is not limited to a loss due to death. We grieve losing a job, a relationship, moving to a new city, basically any change to our lives results in a grieving process. What is missed is how quickly some grieving takes us to a place of acceptance. If one were to save up to buy a new car and junk an older rust bucket they've been driving, chances are getting to a place of acceptance would happen very quickly, happy with their new ride.

On the other hand, if a child moved to a new city but loved where the family lived before, enjoyed the school, and had lots of friends, they would live in grief for quite a bit longer. The moving transaction removes confidence and could make someone feel less authentic if their identity had deep connections to where they previously lived. This doesn't suggest it's good or bad, but merely a truth one uses to express their identity.

While actively seeking deposits is beneficial, it doubles down by steering us away from pitfalls.

Excessive reliance on external validation can make our emotional balance volatile. It's essential to balance seeking external affirmations and sound internal self-belief. Over time, the goal should be to make more substantial internal deposits and enforce that our self-worth and confidence are not overly contingent on external factors or being codependent. The landscape of our lives is ever evolving, with its ups and downs. By distinguishing between the sources of our emotional deposits and actively immersing with them, grieving when needed, we can ensure a favorable balance in our Identity ATM to draw from. Two central guides to our steps toward validation are the pulse of the present moment and the beckoning allure of the future. Being present is a heartfelt experience, an immersion into the fabric of the here and now, occupying our current realities, emotions, and surroundings. On the other hand, forward-thinking is the art of anticipation, planning, and envisioning what lies ahead. Striking a balance between these two can be challenging but essential for a fulfilling life.

Being present, or mindfulness as it is often termed has its roots in ancient practices. It emphasizes living in the moment, free from the distractions of past regrets or future anxieties. When we are genuinely present, we experience life in its purest form. We listen more attentively, observe more keenly, and commit more deeply. This engagement with our experiences deepens our relationships and grounds us in a reality often lost in the hustle and bustle of modern life.

However, being immersed in the present without thinking about the future can be limiting. It might result in missed opportunities, lack of preparedness, or stagnation. This is where forward-thinking comes into play. The compass guides us toward our aspirations, dreams, and goals. Being forward-thinking means we are proactive, planning for future endeavors and setting the stage for success. It's about admitting that while the present is fleeting, our actions today have long-lasting implications for tomorrow.

Yet, an overemphasis on forward-thinking can have its pitfalls. Constantly living in the future might prompt anxiety, missing out on the joys of today, and even feelings of perpetual dissatisfaction, as the future can always paint a picture of something better, bigger, or brighter.

The art lies in balancing these two perspectives. It's about grounding oneself in the present, savoring each moment while keeping an eye on the horizon, preparing, and planning for what's to come. Such a balance shows that we are not just reactive beings, swayed by the winds of time, but also proactive architects of our destiny.

In essence, the cognitive tension between being present and forward-thinking is delicate. It requires auditing our thoughts and continuously reviewing how they are processed. Embracing these perspectives makes the most of each moment while paving the way for a future that resonates with our dreams and aspirations. In this balance lies the beauty of a well-lived life, where every step is grounded in the now and stepping into the promise of tomorrow.

Every day dispenses opportunities for emotional deposits. Whether it's a small gesture of kindness, achieving a personal goal, or simply accepting our worth, these deposits accumulate. Over time, they create a reservoir of emotional wealth, substantiating that we maneuver through life with resilience and grace. As we progress through this book, we will explore the various ways to secure this wealth, embarking on a fulfilling emotional journey.

Questions for Reflection:

1. What specific event or situation triggers guilt or shame, and why are those emotions associated with those events?
2. How do these feelings of guilt or shame manifest in my behavior, relationships, and self-perception?
3. What underlying beliefs or values, such as guilt or shame, might influence my reactions?
4. In what ways might I be holding onto guilt or shame that no longer serves a purpose or aligns with my current growth projection?
5. How can I approach these feelings with compassion, and what steps can I take to heal or reconcile with these emotions?

The Identity ATM

Identity Withdrawals: The Cost of Guilt and Shame

Chapter Concept: When life transactions are processed constructively, guilt can foster growth, responsibility, and empathy. Unchecked shame develops into self-loathing, alienation, and a distorted self-image.

Chapter Strategy for Enrichment: Enhance the Identity ATM's processes to filter guilt and shame proactively.

Life is seldom linear. Just as there are moments that bolster our emotional wealth, there are instances that test it, retrieving funds from our Identity ATM. Guilt and shame are two of the most potent emotional forces that can instigate these withdrawals. Not all transactions with the Identity ATM are positive.

Specific experiences lead to emotional withdrawals, draining our self-worth. Validating these moments and their origins can prevent emotional bankruptcy, which would result in shame rather than guilt.

At their core, guilt and shame are mechanisms for exploration. They signal a misalignment between actions and values. Guilt, often described as a 'feeling of having done wrong,' is a response to a specific action, often regretted. It acknowledges that we've stepped out of line with our moral compass. Guilt serves as a mirror, reflecting deeper truths about our lives. At its core, guilt arises when we perceive a misalignment between our actions and moral or ethical standards. This incongruence highlights areas of our lives where we may feign in alignment with our values. Sometimes, guilt points to unresolved conflicts, unmet responsibilities, or suppressed desires. For example, feeling guilty about not spending enough time with loved ones may reveal deeper truths about our priorities and time allocation. Guilt stemming from not standing up for oneself might indicate underlying issues of self-worth and assertiveness. When embraced introspectively, guilt becomes more than just an uncomfortable emotion; it transforms into a compass, pointing out areas of our lives that require attention, introspection, and, potentially, change. In this light, guilt can be seen not merely as a burden but as a tool for self-awareness and growth, guiding us closer to our authentic selves and life more congruent with our deepest values.

More intense than guilt, shame is not just about what we did but who we are. It's an internal belief that something is fundamentally wrong with us, making us unworthy of love, connection, or belonging. Shame wants to force upon someone a change in how they express their identity, misguiding that person's self-awareness into believing they are not who they thought they were. While both emotions serve as self-regulatory mechanisms, unchecked guilt and shame can be devastating in probability, severity, and frequency.

The issue with shame is that it pretends to be a bank, and shame is very good at pretending. I remember calling my actual bank once, and the verification process asked for my social security number, my email address linked to my account, my phone number linked to my account, a text message verification code, and the account number itself. It wasn't a scam, either. Shame, however, is a scam and will put you through the emotional and mental ringer to the most critical point of questioning your own identity. If someone expresses their problem with alcohol abuse, the Identity ATM defers this to be an expression of their identity rooted in shame, where the real problem lies. The problem isn't the alcohol but the relationship with their own identity. Shame always wants to focus on the expression of one's identity, not one's identity itself.

Once shame has you questioning your own true self, it begins to double down on the damaging work exactly where it needs you to be – isolated, alone, wondering if how you coped with issues has been a true reflection of yourself. The Identity ATM framework would suggest that while enduring a trial, there is an underlying impact on your identity to consider. Without bringing attention to how it is impacting you, the risk of confusion and mental chaos increases exponentially.

The Fees for Emotional Withdrawals

The fees on emotional withdrawals aren't always immediate. They can be gradual, eroding our self-worth over time. Conceding the triggers and patterns of these withdrawals is the first step toward mitigation and, eventually, elimination of dangerous expressions of our identity. They are often no different than ATM fees, payments made due to transactions we can't avoid. For example, a child growing up in an abusive home or simply being around indirect abuse.

Expressions like rumination, constantly replaying adverse events in our minds, amplify feelings of guilt and shame. This chronic overthinking can deplete our emotional reserves. Isolation and withdrawal from social connections compound the negative emotions, further draining our emotional bank. Self-criticism brings harsh self-judgment, along with emotional withdrawals. Regularly belittling or doubting oneself can have a compounding effect on our emotional balance.

Traumatic experiences often result in swift and severe emotional withdrawals. Imagine logging into your bank account only to see that your funds have been completely depleted. Trauma presents a similar dynamic to our psyche, such as identity theft. You are left feeling you're you, but not "the you" you know yourself to be. The choice then becomes a matter of how to respond. With no support to process trauma, they are likely to engage in destructive behavior, isolate or ignore the pain, perhaps even displace their pain, or seek to heal or destroy someone else. It isn't until the person experiencing the impact of trauma learns how to live in the truth of their situation that the healing process begins.

Trauma, an intense psychological response to distressing events, leaves indelible imprints on the psyche. Often, when individuals endure traumatic experiences, they not only grapple with the immediate pain and shock but also, quite frequently, with lingering feelings of guilt and shame. Deeply rooted in human cognition and self-perception, these emotions amplify healing and recovery.

An interesting dynamic of counseling is how counselees want to define their terms. The interplay between science and experience is not lost here, especially when using terms like trauma or depression. Some may truly believe their experience is traumatic, even if it does not fall within the psychologist or psychiatrist's clinical definition. This illuminates the need to seek professional counseling. Every discussion should start with defining your terms. What do you mean, and what does your therapist mean when the term trauma or depression is used? How is shame defined in the context of your conversation?

The explicit goal of the Identity ATM here is to encourage reading from specialists in the fields that relate to your mental and emotional health, allowing the Identity ATM to provide the framework to process what you're learning. For example, to familiarize oneself with the interplay between guilt and shame, it's indispensable to first differentiate between these two emotions. Guilt typically arises when individuals believe they've done something wrong. It is associated with a specific event or action and often prompts a desire to make amends. In contrast, shame is a more pervasive emotion. It is not merely about feeling wrong about something one did but feeling bad about who one is—an acute sense of worthlessness or being flawed at a fundamental level. When traumatic events unfold, especially in situations where individuals feel they have a role to play (even if they objectively did not), guilt can manifest. For example, survivors of accidents might irrationally feel guilty for having survived when others didn't, a phenomenon often termed "survivor's guilt." They may ruminate over what they could have done differently, even if, rationally, they know they had no control over the outcome. This self-blame becomes a means, albeit maladaptive, to regain a semblance of control over the uncontrollable.

Similarly, victims of abuse, particularly in prolonged situations like domestic violence or childhood maltreatment, might internalize feelings of guilt. They may wrongly believe they did something to provoke the abuse or could have done something to prevent it. Victims sometimes believe they deserve the abuse. Recurring exposure to such traumatic situations can warp self-perception. This transition from guilt to shame is heartbreaking, as the individual doesn't just grieve the harm done to them but also begins to see themselves as inherently deserving of such harm.

Shame, particularly in the aftermath of trauma, can be exceptionally debilitating. It breeds in silence and isolation. Many victims, cloaked in the shadows of shame, refrain from sharing their experiences, fearing judgment or further ostracization. This silence perpetuates the cycle of trauma, as the lack of open dialogue and support can hinder healing and potentially expose the individual to harm further. The numerous responses to shame include submitting to a fear-based outlook on life, which provides for anger and a lack of trust in support systems, as well as substance abuse with whatever vice is limiting a person's ability to move beyond shame.

Culture and societal norms shape these reactions. In many societies, there exists a tendency to blame victims for the traumatic events they endure. Whether it's the stigma attached to mental health struggles, the blame apportioned to victims of sexual assault based on their attire or behavior, or the judgment passed on those in abusive relationships for not leaving sooner, these societal reactions intensify feelings of guilt and shame. In essence, the trauma is not just in the event but is perpetuated by societal responses.

Furthermore, the brain's mechanisms in the aftermath of trauma can exacerbate feelings of guilt and shame. Traumatic events change areas of the brain like the amygdala, which governs fear, and the prefrontal cortex, which is involved in decision-making. These changes can result in heightened states of alertness, anxiety, and rumination. In this heightened state, individuals may continuously replay the traumatic event, each time scrutinizing their actions, which further ingrains feelings of guilt and shame.

Yet, this nexus of trauma, guilt, and shame also illuminates pathways to healing. Recognizing that these feelings of guilt and shame are, in many instances, misplaced and result from psychological, societal, and neurological factors can be liberating. Professional therapies, such as cognitive-behavioral therapy, can be instrumental in challenging and reframing these self-blaming beliefs. Additionally, trauma-informed care, which deciphers the widespread impact of trauma and integrates this survey into therapy, can be particularly effective.

Group therapies and support groups offer another avenue of healing. Here, individuals share their experiences, breaking the silence that shame often imposes. Listening to others and sharing realized feelings can diminish the isolation that trauma survivors often feel, allowing them to see that they are not alone in their struggles.

The relationship between trauma, guilt, and shame is deeply interwoven into our identity. Traumatic events disrupt the equilibrium of our lives by their very nature. When compounded by guilt and shame, the journey to recovery becomes even more challenging. This interplay, challenging societal norms perpetuating victim-blaming, and seeking supportive therapeutic environments can pave the way for healing. While trauma leaves scars, addressing the associated guilt and shame can transform these scars into symbols of resilience and strength.

Guilt, Shame, and Society

Our environment and cultural backdrop mold our encounters with guilt and shame. Every culture has its set of unwritten rules. Transgressions, even if unintentional, can drive feelings of guilt. In some cultures, these transgressions might also be linked to shame, affecting the individual and their family. In today's digital age, comparisons are more rampant than ever. Feelings of inadequacy or shame about not measuring up may be the fallout to seeing peers achieve milestones you wanted for yourself. Childhood experiences have lasting impacts, as it is when an enormous number of subconscious vows are made. Unrealistic expectations or conditional love from caregivers can sow seeds of guilt and shame, which might persist into adulthood.

Navigating Emotional Withdrawals

Understanding is half the battle. Discovering the sources and patterns of emotional withdrawals, we can develop strategies to address them more effectively. Reframing Thoughts: Cognitive restructuring, a cognitive-behavioral therapy (CBT) technique, can be instrumental. By challenging and altering negative thought patterns, we can mitigate the impact of guilt and shame. Shame thrives in secrecy. By opening and sharing our feelings with trusted individuals, we can break the cycle of isolation. Such connections often apply to feelings of empathy, which can counteract the effects of shame. Practicing self-compassion involves treating ourselves with the same kindness we would a friend. This approach can be a balm for the wounds inflicted by guilt and shame. Sometimes, the depth of guilt and shame can be overwhelming. In such cases, seeking therapy or counseling can provide structured support and coping mechanisms.

The Role of Forgiveness

Forgiveness towards oneself and others is a powerful tool against the debilitating effects of guilt and shame. We can reduce the magnitude of emotional withdrawals by conceding our human fallibility and extending compassion. This involves observing our mistakes, taking corrective actions, and moving forward without incessant self-punishment. Holding onto grudges or resentments can extend to feelings of guilt and shame. By forgiving others, we free ourselves from these emotional chains.

As the introduction describes, much of our ability to forgive depends on who we bank with. Our faith, family, or current context shapes how we do certain things, and forgiving ourselves or someone else is often learned from our bank. Our heritage and culture impact numerous aspects of our personal and interpersonal lives. One such dimension substantially influenced by cultural nuances is the act of forgiveness. How we approach transgressions, the concept of redemption, and extend or withhold forgiveness often have deeply embedded cultural underpinnings.

Many cultures exalt the virtue of forgiveness, equating it with moral superiority and strength of character. For instance, numerous religious traditions, from the banks of faith, such as Christianity's teachings to Buddhism's emphasis on compassion, promote forgiveness as a virtuous act. In such cultures, there might be societal pressure to forgive, sometimes even when the individual is not ready to relinquish the act of forgiveness that isn't a genuine emotional release. Conversely, some cultures might equate forgiveness with weakness, positing that it invites further transgressions or denotes an inability to stand up for oneself. In these contexts, holding onto grudges or seeking retribution is seen as a more appropriate response, potentially exacerbating cycles of conflict and mistrust.

Furthermore, societal stigmas and taboos influence the spectrum of forgiveness. Certain acts are deemed unforgivable in many cultures due to their heinous nature or contradiction to core societal values. This categorization, while sometimes valid, can also hinder individual agency in the process of forgiveness.

The Role of Mercy

The insights associated with mercy should be noticed, too. As the need for self-forgiveness increases, so does the need for self-compassion. Mercy is the self-compassion because it holds the proper authority to lessen the severity of punishment. Mercy brings the balance of power back from the depths of shame. Mercy is positioned as a power dynamic in the emotional work of the psyche. While mercy and forgiveness have different functions with the Identity ATM, mercy supports forgiveness' ability to let go of resentment, anger, and revenge-seeking agendas.

The frameworks and corresponding interplay between mercy and forgiveness mitigate the harm involved. Mercy and forgiveness are approachable in the Identity ATM. They signify a willingness not just to change but to transcend justice in favor of compassion and a reciprocal opening toward reconciliation.

Forgiveness does not always change the outcome for the offender as much as it changes the internal landscape of the one who has been wronged, leaving it as a more cathartic release and unburdening of the soul compared to the reduced judgment that mercy extends.

Inspecting these cultural nuances is the first step in unpacking and potentially unlearning them. Unlearning doesn't necessarily mean discarding cultural values but involves critically examining them to determine which ones align with personal beliefs and which ones don't. Here are steps to contend with this unlearning process:

Self-reflection: Take some time to peruse your personal beliefs regarding forgiveness. Try to analyze your thoughts and feelings towards this concept and consider how it may affect your relationships with others. What feels right, and what feels imposed? Journaling, meditation, or discussions can be tools to aid this process.

Educate oneself: Learn about different cultural and philosophical perspectives on forgiveness and mercy. This broadens horizons via alternative viewpoints, aiding informed decisions.

Seek guidance: Therapists, counselors, or spiritual leaders trained in culturally informed practices may share insights into how culture impacts forgiveness patterns and offer tools to direct them toward promising outcomes and the differences mercy opens you to.

Engage in dialogue: Open discussions about forgiveness and mercy, within communities or with diverse groups, can break down culturally imposed silos and forge against listening to one another with less or no judgment.

Practice empathy: Appreciate that the journey is deeply personal. While cultural norms can guide, they shouldn't dictate. Everyone's path is unique and valid.

While being a guiding force, your culture doesn't have to be binding. When one thought that was once a protective boundary becomes a barrier preventing growth, it is time to reassess why it was established as a boundary. Sensing its influence within our posture toward forgiveness, it chooses a path that resonates with our truths, championing genuine healing and reconciliation.

The Ripple Effect of Withdrawals

Unchecked emotional withdrawals can have cascading effects on various aspects of our lives. Reduced self-worth can impact our decision-making, risk-taking ability, and interpersonal relationships. Over time, chronic feelings of guilt and shame culminate in mental health concerns like depression, anxiety, and chronic stress.

Despite their challenging nature, experiences of guilt and shame can serve as catalysts for growth. They push us to introspect, reassess, and recalibrate. After grappling with these emotions, many individuals emerge more resilient, empathetic, and self-aware. The key lies in constructive collaboration with these feelings rather than suppression or avoidance. The experience of forgiveness, redemption, and subsequent growth is, in essence, the result of grieving.

The Role of Grief

Grief, an emotional response to loss, often paints the human experience with shades of melancholy, despair, and confusion. While it's traditionally associated with the death of a loved one, grief isn't limited to that. It accompanies various pivotal moments in our lives, from the end of adored relationships to shifts in personal identities, from job losses to moving away from a beloved hometown. Each change, each ending, ushers in its unique form of grief. Yet, within these emotions' labyrinth lies a path leading to personal growth, strength, and a deeper grasp of oneself and the world.

When one confronts grief, the first realization often revolves around its complexity. It isn't a singular, static emotion. Instead, it's a spectrum, a journey. The well-documented stages of grief—denial, anger, bargaining, depression, and acceptance—proposed by psychiatrist Elisabeth Kübler-Ross serve as a testament to this journey. However, it's paramount to remember that everyone's path through these stages is personal and non-linear. A person may grapple with anger long before they touch the shores of denial or may find themselves oscillating between depression and acceptance. Celebrating this fluidity extends grace to the grieving individual to heal at their own pace, without the burden of societal expectations.

As we filter out the disorienting noise that hinders growth, the introspective moments, the silent pauses, and the quiet assessments matter. Our perspectives undergo a seismic shift in the face of loss. What was once taken for granted might now seem precious. The transient nature of life becomes evident, prompting many to re-evaluate their priorities and values. In this re-evaluation, many find a renewed sense of purpose, a more fervent appreciation for the present, and a deeper commitment to meaningful relationships.

Furthermore, the vulnerability exposed by grief often heightens one's self-awareness. As we confront and process the pain, we come face-to-face with our deepest fears, regrets, desires, and aspirations. This confrontation, while undoubtedly challenging, also catalyzes self-discovery. In assenting to these emotions, we get a clearer picture of who we truly are and what we genuinely value, separate from societal impositions or external validations.

Another transformative aspect of navigating grief is the evolving nature of empathy and compassion. Experiencing grief makes the fragility of human existence palpable. This awareness, in turn, makes us more receptive to the sufferings and joys of others. We begin to forge connections rooted in shared human experiences. The bonds supported during grief, whether with loved ones or even strangers, often possess a depth that stands the test of time.

Grief also fortifies resilience. The journey from the throes of despair to finding a semblance of peace is a testament to the human spirit's indomitable strength. Each step forward, each day where one finds the courage to smile again, to hope again, adds to this reservoir of resilience. Over time, this resilience becomes a beacon, guiding us through subsequent adversities and reminding us of our inherent capacity to heal and rebuild.

Finally, when finding a way through the maze of grief, there's often a keen revelation about the interconnectedness of life. Changes, endings, and beginnings are intrinsically linked. The end of one chapter invariably heralds the beginning of another. By embracing this cyclical nature of life, we open ourselves to new experiences, opportunities, and relationships. The pain of what was lost never truly vanishes, but it's accompanied by gratitude for what was and hope for what's yet to come.

In essence, while grief is an undeniably painful response to changes and losses life presents, it's also a wise teacher. It instructs us about the depths of our emotions, the strength of our spirit, and the beauty of human connection. By embracing the lessons embedded within grief, we honor our losses and bring dignity to the transformation taking place.

The bond between grief and our identity becomes disoriented when in crisis and the ensuing months and years. Depending on how close one is to another, their identity is as much lost as the person that died because they can only see themselves linked to that person or the role they held in the relationship with that person. How many viral stories have you seen where a couple married for decades pass away within a short amount of time from one another? A parent who loses a child may struggle with their identity as a caregiver, while someone who loses their spouse grapples with the loss of being a partner. Individuals grieve based in part on their identity in the loss. Identity certainly influences their grief.

What should be sought out is to determine if the frameworks of grieving within your identity are either supportive or restraining. There are no textbook steps to grieving. You may find yourself in any grief stage at any time. Grief isn't about how to move on with your life but learning how to live with a new set of facts about your life and the relationship your identity will have with those facts from here on out. Guilt and shame, while uncomfortable, are integral components of the human experience of grieving. They serve as reminders of our values and boundaries. However, unchecked, they can lead to major emotional withdrawals, depleting our self-worth and confidence. We can minimize their adverse impacts by comprehending the nuances of these emotions, apprehending their triggers, and adopting constructive coping strategies. As we journey further, we will explore more about balancing these withdrawals with emotional deposits, ensuring a harmonious emotional landscape.

Engaging the following questions can provide insights into guilt and shame's multifaceted impact on one's life. By reducing the cost of these emotions, individuals can begin the journey of healing, self-compassion, and growth.

My encouragement here is to have a professional counselor, or a trusted source support you in answering these questions if you feel or sense the need. All of the material, including the questions, is provided to promote conversation, internal dialogue, journal entries, or even topics to discuss with your therapist. The goal is thought processing to view the account balances in your Identity ATM objectively.

The wealthiest people on the planet have financial advisors to help protect them from risks and dangers. How much more would you consider your identity to be worth? If you decide to seek help, I encourage you to find someone just as curious about your thought processing and decision-making as you are. This isn't about them. It's about you, who you bank with, and how you can benefit from a healthy frame of mind.

Questions for Reflection:

1. What specific moments in my life trigger guilt or shame?
2. How do these feelings of guilt and shame manifest physically, mentally, and emotionally in my daily life?
3. In what ways have guilt or shame influenced my decision-making or choices?
4. Are there opportunities or experiences I've avoided because of underlying guilt or shame?
5. How have persistent feelings of guilt or shame impacted my self-esteem and self-worth?
6. Have I developed any coping mechanisms or habits to deal with grief?
7. Are there patterns or recurring themes that bring about these feelings? Can I identify their origin?
8. How does guilt or shame affect my ability to grieve?
9. How does my societal or cultural context influence my perceptions of guilt and shame? Are there external pressures that exacerbate these feelings?
10. In what ways have I sought help or support in managing these emotions?

Identity Theft: Balancing Deposits against Withdrawals

Chapter Concept: By employing self-reflection, emotional intelligence, and empathy, we can navigate the expressions of guilt and shame.

Chapter Strategy for Enrichment: Recognizing the signposts of our emotional journey, like triggers and patterns, helps in effective navigation.

Our emotional transactions play a pivotal role in identity formation and maintenance. These transactions, comprising both deposits and withdrawals, shape the contours of our self-worth and confidence. A balanced emotional account vouches for holistic well-being. When the balance is not maintained, the result is often a loss of identity, as though someone or something else is determining who we are, making transactions without our awareness or involvement.

Life presents circumstances that profoundly alter our sense of self, akin to identity theft. This metaphorical identity theft occurs in experiences such as trauma and grief, thus forcing us to question or abandon aspects we once held as certain. For example, a career-driven person suddenly facing unemployment for the first time in twenty years might feel as though their very foundation has been stolen from them. This captures everything from their routines to self-perceptions that, to them, defined their daily existence, now all stripped away, leaving them with a void where their identity once was. The same may go for someone facing the end of a long-term relationship or another who loses a physical capability and disconnects from the essence of their able-bodied identity. Identity theft leaves individuals feeling lost, vulnerable, and unsure of who they are or what their purpose is, similar to the disorientation one feels after having their personal details stolen and misused.

The journey back to oneself or the reconstruction of a new, evolved identity is challenging. Every interaction and experience can be viewed as a transaction in our Identity ATM. While some transactions fortify our self-esteem, others confront it. These benefit in this is investment and expenditure transactions earn interest in our emotional wealth little by little. Over time, our emotional net worth frees us from burdens and allows us to emerge with a deeper, more nuanced identity. If we are somehow deceived by others or lie to ourselves because we don't want to accept truth, we are opening ourselves up to identity theft.

The risk of self-deception, identity theft in this book's context, amplifies the need to invest in healthier emotional lives. Just like financial investments, emotional investments should be properly researched before you go all in. Investing in positive affirmations, self-care routines, and constructive endeavors can yield rich dividends in self-worth and confidence. Where we allocate our resources with the hope of returns, we are making emotional investments. These may be investments in people, experiences, and even our dreams. This process, deeply personal and often intuitive, impacts our well-being, shapes our interpersonal behavior, and dictates the course of our life's journey.

When we speak of emotional investments, we refer to the energy, time, and feelings we invest in something or someone. It's an active choice, even if subconscious at times, determining where we place our emotional attention. The genesis of such investments often lies in our innate desire for connection and meaning. We yearn for bonds, shared experiences, and moments that resonate deeply with our core. Therefore, we invest emotionally in relationships, friendships, passions, and causes that align with our values and aspirations.

As with any investment, the emotional kind also comes with risks and rewards. The rewards are palpable: a relationship that blossoms over time, friendships that stand the test of adversity, passions that give a sense of purpose, or causes that bring about real change. These positive returns provide validation, a sense of belonging, and, often, wholehearted joy. They reinforce our choices and motivate us to continue investing in and honoring ourselves.

On the flip side, the risks are equally real. Not all emotional investments yield positive returns. Sometimes, relationships falter, friendships wane, passion becomes burnout, and causes morph into disillusionment. The cost of such investments gone awry is high, with byproducts of disappointment, betrayal, or heartbreak. The emotional toll can be prominent, leading to periods of introspection, doubt, and even withdrawal.

Therefore, the art of making wise emotional investments hinges on a delicate balance. It requires self-awareness and the ability to discern where to invest and where to hold back. Absorbing your emotional needs, boundaries, and capacity is paramount. Just as a savvy investor analyzes market trends, risks, and potential returns before putting money into a venture, you must also utilize introspection, evaluation, and sometimes even seek counsel before delving deep into emotional commitments.

It's also worth noting that the nature of emotional investments evolves with time. As we journey through different life stages, our priorities and needs and emotional investments change. The friendships we deeply invested in during our school days might not hold the same place in our lives in our thirties. The passions we pursued fervently in our youth might give way to newer interests as we age. This evolution is natural and is a testament to our growth, learning, and the transient nature of life itself.

Another aspect of this process is how emotional investments are transactional. Unlike financial investments, where the expectation of a return is explicit, emotional investments thrive as they become implicit. The intent isn't to receive more praise but to cherish a categorically wholeness to our identity. However, this isn't finite and doesn't negate the need for reciprocity in relationships or the pursuit of passions that resonate deeply.

Emotional investments are the lifeblood of our human experience. They add depth to our relationships, passion to our pursuits, and purpose to our existence. While they come with uncertainties, the potential for growth, connection, and joy makes the journey worthwhile. By giving and receiving, a type of investing and divesting, we enrich our lives and feed into human connection and experience.

Emotional Expenditures

In the ecosystem of human emotions, where investments and returns are often discussed, another facet demands our attention: emotional expenditures. This refers to the vibrant energy we spend in our day-to-day lives, whether in response to external circumstances or our internal dialogues. Mentally registering these expenditures directly influences our emotional well-being, resilience, and capacity to connect and thrive.

Emotional expenditures occur in various forms. We spend emotional energy when we embrace a challenging conversation, cope with disappointment, or grapple with relationships. These expenditures are akin to withdrawals from an emotional bank account. Daily stressors, like traffic jams, work deadlines, or even a minor disagreement with a loved one, are taking small withdrawals from our Identity ATM. Larger, more influential events, like a personal loss, a career setback, or a betrayal, result in more substantial deductions from our emotional reserves.

As with any account, if the withdrawals or, in this case, emotional expenditures, outpace the deposits, we risk running into a deficit. An emotional deficiency manifests as exhaustion, burnout, detachment, or even ailments like anxiety and depression. It's a state where our emotional resilience is compromised, and our ability to cope with further stressors is diminished.

It's also pertinent to mention that not all emotional expenditures are negative. Celebratory events, such as weddings, achievements, or milestones, can be emotionally taxing. They, too, require emotional energy, albeit in a joyful context. The expenditure in these situations is feelings of fulfillment, gratitude, and contentment. But they still deplete our emotional reserves and necessitate replenishment.

To manage emotional expenditures effectively, the first step is awareness. Distinguishing when and where we spend our emotional energy helps us set boundaries, prioritize self-care, and seek support when needed. It's akin to tracking expenses in a financial budget so one does not overspend and go bankrupt.

Furthermore, the nature of our emotional expenditures can also illuminate patterns in our behaviors and choices.

For instance, if we repeatedly find ourselves drained after interactions with a particular individual or group, it might be worth reassessing the relationship. If specific tasks or situations at work consistently matriculate into emotional burnout, it might be time to discuss changes or consider alternatives.

Moreover, balancing emotional expenditures requires intentional actions to recharge. Just as financial stability is achieved by balancing spending with earning, emotional equilibrium is maintained by complementing expenditures with rejuvenating activities. This could mean indulging in hobbies, practicing meditation, seeking therapy, or spending quality time with loved ones. It's about identifying what fills up our emotional reserves and advocating that we make time for it.

Another aspect of managing emotional expenditures is building and maintaining a support system. Just as businesses often have contingency funds for unexpected expenses, having a reliable support system. That is comprised of friends, family, or professionals is a safety net for unforeseen emotional expenditures. They offer perspective, security, and a listening ear, all of which can mitigate the impact of emotional drain.

Emotional expenditures are deeply personal and ever evolving. It's the ebb and flow of spending and replenishing. Conceding the nuances of evolving and life's rhythms and taking proactive steps to maintain balance bolsters emotional stability and a richer, more fulfilling life experience. As we become astute managers of our emotional expenditures, we pave the way for growth, deeper connections, and a contextualization of the self and the world around us. Emotional payments show the many ways life is replete with tests of our emotional resilience. These can range from personal setbacks to external criticisms. Managing these expenditures without depleting our emotional reserves is key.

Overdrawn Situations

Just like in banking, it's possible to overdraw from our emotional accounts. Chronic feelings of inadequacy, hopelessness, or overwhelming guilt and shame characterize an overdrawn emotional state. Seeing the signs is the first step toward recovery. Persistent self-doubt, constantly questioning one's worth, capabilities, or decisions, can indicate an overdrawn state. Evading social interactions, responsibilities, or potential criticism is another sign. Sometimes, there are even physical manifestations, such as chronic fatigue, sleep disturbances, or unexplained aches, which can sometimes be indicative of an overdrawn emotional state.

Strategies for Balancing Transactions

One must proactively manage deposits and withdrawals to maintain a balanced emotional account. Actions one could enlist in for balancing transactions are self-care, boundary setting, and taking time with inner dialogue.

Self-care involves setting aside time for activities that rejuvenate and refresh, whether meditation, hobbies, or simply resting. Regularly affirming one's worth through self-talk or seeking positive environments protects a steady flow of deposits. Instead of avoiding feedback, actively seeking it and using it for growth can prevent feelings of guilt and shame. In the relentless pace of modern life, the art of self-care emerges as a sanctuary, a quiet corner of respite where we turn inwards to confront our weary souls. Far from indulgence, self-care is an essential practice, a testament to our inherent worth, and an endorsement of our human need to replenish and rejuvenate.

Self-care is going beyond the popularized spa days or luxury retreats. At its core, it's about honoring our mental, emotional, physical, and spiritual needs. It's the whisper of the early morning breeze during a solitary walk, the cathartic release of a heartfelt journal entry, or the restorative power of a night of deep sleep. Every act, big or small, that aligns with our innermost needs furnishes a healthy manner of self-care.

Physical self-care might mean honoring our bodies through movement through a dance class, a jog in the park, or the gentle stretches of yoga. It's also about nourishing ourselves with foods that fuel our bodies, listening to their signals of fatigue or restlessness, and granting them rest when needed. However, self-care extends beyond the tangible realm. Emotionally, it's about setting boundaries, obtaining feelings without judgment, and seeking spaces and relationships that feed positivity.

Mentally, self-care challenges negative thought patterns in activities that stimulate the mind and occasionally disconnects from the constant barrage of digital information. It's about seeking clarity, embracing moments of stillness, and, when necessary, seeking professional guidance addressing the mind's entanglements.

Spiritually, self-care transcends religious confines, becoming a quest for meaning, purpose, and connection. Whether it's through meditation, prayer, nature walks, or philosophical discussions, it's about connecting with something more splendid, finding solace in the vastness of the universe, and grounding ourselves in our beliefs and values.

Yet, in the discourse on self-care, remember that it's deeply personal. This solace and rejuvenation to one might not resonate with another. The essence lies in introspection, what our soul craves, and honoring those needs without guilt or hesitation.

Positioning self-care as a priority is a revolutionary act in a world that often demands relentless output. It's an affirmation of our worth, a statement that we matter. By weaving self-care into the fabric of our daily lives, we enhance our well-being and equip ourselves with grace, resilience, and an enduring spirit.

Boundary setting is being clear about what we can tolerate emotionally, which helps in preventing undue withdrawals. This includes distancing oneself from toxic relationships or environments. The act of setting boundaries emerges as an essential choreography. It's about marking the spaces where we begin and where the external world ends, trekking along our path with clarity, respect, and self-assurance. Both visible and invisible boundaries shape our experiences, direct our energies, and delineate our realms of comfort and safety.

At the heart of setting boundaries lies self-awareness. Our needs, desires, limits, and vulnerabilities define what we can tolerate and what's non-negotiable. These boundaries might pertain to our time, emotional energy, personal space, values, and beliefs. When we have clear boundaries, we permit ourselves to say 'no' without guilt and to ask for what we need without hesitation.

Yet, the task isn't just about setting boundaries; it's also about communicating them effectively. Clear communication doubles down that those around us respect our limits. It prevents misunderstandings, resentment, and conflicts. But it's equally essential to express these boundaries with compassion and assertiveness, striking a balance that neither alienates nor diminishes our stance.

However, as essential as setting boundaries is, it's often met with resistance. The world, accustomed to unlimited access, might push back and label us as 'difficult' or 'selfish.' In such moments, the fortitude to uphold our boundaries becomes paramount. It's a testament to our self-respect, signaling that we prioritize our well-being and worth.

Setting boundaries is not about isolating ourselves or building impenetrable walls. It's about creating a safe space to thrive, connect, and engage. While they may seem like barriers, these boundaries are, in fact, bridges. They bridge the gap between our authentic selves and the external world in every interaction rooted in respect and mutual appreciation. By mastering the art of developing boundaries, we enhance the quality of our interactions and relationships. Thus, they become the framework within which the beautiful mosaic of our lives takes shape, filled with colors of respect, dignity, and self-love.

Internal contemplation and journaling are setting aside time to clarify the connections amidst one's actions, feelings, and experiences. Journaling these deliberations can be therapeutic and enlightening. In the quiet corners of our minds, amidst the din of daily life, lies a reservoir of thoughts, emotions, and experiences that yearn for expression. Often, they remain suppressed or unexplored, buried beneath the strains of our routines. The practices are powerful tools for healing, learning, and personal growth.

Journaling is akin to a heartfelt conversation with oneself. As the pen glides across the paper, it unravels layers of emotions, sheds light on buried memories, and articulates thoughts that might have seemed nebulous. Transcribing our inner world creates a tangible record of our journey and insights into patterns, desires, and fears that might have previously eluded our consciousness. Over time, as we revisit these pages, we trace our evolution and find a sense of closure regarding past events.

On the other hand, searching one's soul is a more profound process. It invites us to pause and give space for our experiences to breathe, to question the 'whys' and 'hows' of our actions and reactions. This act of contemplation aids in detangling and deconstructing our emotions, discerning the root causes of our joys, sorrows, anxieties, and contentment. It's an inward journey that yields self-awareness, revealing our triggers, strengths, and growth areas.

Together, they form a symbiotic relationship. While journaling supplies an outlet, a safe space to pour out without judgment, reflection adds depth, helping us discern the landscapes of our psyche with a discerning lens. This combined process becomes therapeutic, a self-led healing journey that grants clarity, catharsis, and a deeper connection to our proper selves. Moreover, as we consistently invest in these practices, we inadvertently promote a habit of mindfulness. We become attuned to our emotions and thoughts as they arise, learning to address them rather than letting them fester. This proactive approach to mental and emotional well-being aids in preempting potential emotional upheavals. It is also a mechanism to cope more resiliently.

The inner search anchors us in a world that often emphasizes external achievements and validations. They remind us of the significance of the inner journey, of the transformative power of self-dialogue. By forging a relationship with ourselves through these practices, we find healing and embark on a lifelong journey of self-discovery, growth, and discerning inner peace, should those be the values of where you bank. Remember, our identity is heavily influenced by who or what makes deposits into our thoughts and feelings.

Emotional Savings - Building Resilience

True resilience from the Identity ATM perspective is not only the ability to bounce back from adversities but also the ability to learn from the adversity. It's akin to having savings in a bank, which can be used in challenging times. Building emotional resilience ensures that our core self-worth remains unshaken even in the face of withdrawals. Exposing oneself to diverse experiences, even if tough, builds resilience over time. Having a reliable support system, be it family, friends, or support groups, envisions a safety net should emotional downturns take place.

Resilience is an appreciated human quality and has become paramount in today's fast-paced, unpredictable world. Rather than being an innate trait, resilience combines skills and qualities that can be developed over time. The journey of life, filled with its ups and downs, tests our emotional, mental, and sometimes even physical resilience. From personal tragedies to everyday disappointments, resilience acts as our shield, withstanding trials and growing from them.

To begin with, think of the nature of resilience. It does not mean avoiding stress or living a life too carefree. Instead, it signifies experiencing, confronting, and recovering from those challenges. It's facing life head-on, its unpredictable nature, and developing response mechanisms. Resilience is often visualized as a person's ability to stand firm in a storm or to be like a willow tree, flexible and adaptive, bending with the wind but not breaking.

Building resilience is like building a muscle. It requires consistent effort, the right practices, and the principles that strengthen it. Over time, with effort and intention, our resilience muscle can become one of our most robust assets. One of the foundational pillars of resilience is engaging in emotional and mental muscle-building. Emotional responses and triggers, while being in tune with feelings, build resilience. This self-awareness allows us to address emotions head-on, such as fear, anxiety, or sadness, rather than letting them simmer beneath the surface.

Connected to self-awareness is self-care. It's not just a buzzword; it's a fundamental element of resilience. Taking care of our mental, emotional, spiritual, and physical fitness preserves the energy and stamina for life's roadblocks. Regular exercise, a balanced diet, sufficient sleep, and mindfulness practices like meditation enhance our resilience.

Another cornerstone of resilience is maintaining a balanced perspective. Life will always have its ups and downs. Our perspective determines whether we view burdens as insurmountable obstacles or opportunities for growth. It helps reframe setbacks and see them in the broader context of life's journey, establishing a supportive network.

In our moments of distress, having that robust support system can make all the difference. The Identity ATM value system created here is similar to a low or no-interest loan that may be utilized immediately. These support systems serve as lifelines, reminding us that we are not alone in our struggles.

Being proactive is a powerful tool in the resilience-building arsenal. Being assertive involves foreseeing potential problems and preparing for them. This could be in the form of acquiring new skills, seeking knowledge, or developing coping strategies. Setting clear boundaries, as previously discussed, is fundamental to emotional resilience. In an age of constant connectivity and countless responsibilities, knowing when to say no, when to take a break, and when to seek help to maintain our emotional and mental equilibrium trumps momentary desires. These boundaries, professional or personal, outline ways not to spread ourselves too thin and ratify our integrity and sense of self in the face of external pressures. In tandem with setting boundaries is the principle of adaptability. The world is in constant flux, and our ability to adapt to these changes consequentially impacts our resilience. Being open to change, willing to learn, and flexible in our approaches helps us participate in life's unpredictability with grace and gives meaning to it all.

Gratitude, often overlooked, is deeply involved in our resilience. Focusing on what we have rather than what we lack can shift our mindset from scarcity to abundance. Maintaining a gratitude journal or simply taking a few moments each day to appreciate our blessings can enhance our mood, reduce stress, and buffer against life's unpredictable twists and turns. All of these factors into our emotional resilience.

Furthermore, embracing failure as a part of the journey is essential. Every setback, every failure, holds a lesson. Instead of ruminating over what went wrong, resilient individuals analyze these experiences, learn from them, and use them as stepping stones for future endeavors.

Lastly, maintaining a sense of purpose can be the north star in our resilience journey. When we have clarity of purpose, setbacks are seen in the larger context of our life's mission. Whether connected to personal goals, professional aspirations, or broader societal contributions, this purpose provides motivation and direction, especially in challenging times.

Building resilience is an intentional endeavor. It's about equipping ourselves with the tools, mindset, and practices to face them head-on. Feeding our resilience enhances our ability to navigate life's unpredictability and augment our overall well-being, happiness, and fulfillment. In an ever evolving and unpredictable world, resilience is a desirable and essential quality. By relating to its nuances and actively cultivating it, we empower ourselves to face life with grace, tenacity, and an unwavering spirit.

The Compounding Effect

In finance, compound interest on a loan or deposit refers to adding interest to the principal sum. Similarly, consistent deposits carry a compounding effect in emotional banking, where our self-worth and confidence grow exponentially over time. Habit Building, incorporating small, daily habits that add to our emotional wealth, brings long-term benefits. Celebrating small wins can boost our confidence and create a positive feedback loop. Continuous engagements with positive communities, be it interest groups, therapy sessions, or support groups, ensure a steady flow of emotional deposits. Eventually, accumulating small victories becomes a more extensive overarching posture that reflects the transformation of one's identity expressions.

The universe, humanity, and society, however, you want to frame it, operate on a set of principles that, when understood, can illuminate the patterns of our lives. Among these principles, the compounding effect stands out as a silent influencer, guiding trajectories and shaping destinies. The compounding effect embodies the idea that small, seemingly insignificant actions preside over disproportionate outcomes when repeated consistently over time.

Imagine a snowflake gently descending onto a mountaintop. Alone, it's ethereal, fragile, and seemingly inconsequential. However, as more snowflakes fall, gathering slowly over days, months, and years, they amass into a vast snowfield. This accumulation, driven by each snowflake, can give rise to majestic glaciers that carve valleys and shape landscapes. This transformation, though gradual, is a testament to the power of consistency and accumulation. In human endeavors, the compounding effect is ever-present, though often overlooked in favor of immediate gratification. Consider the journey of mastering a craft. The novice artist, writer, or musician doesn't achieve mastery overnight. It's the daily dedication to the art, the consistent practice sessions, and the unyielding passion that, over time, compound into expertise and mastery. Each brush stroke, each penned word, and each musical note plays its part, and their collective influence over time is what births a maestro.

Financial realms are also no strangers to this principle. The world of investments often reveres the magic of compound interest, where the returns generated on an initial sum, when reinvested, cause exponential growth over extended periods. When coupled with the power of compound interest, a modest savings habit can transform into substantial wealth, highlighting consistent, incremental growth.

Yet, the compounding effect isn't exclusive to positive endeavors. Neglect, complacency, and harmful habits can also compound over time with detrimental outcomes. A pattern of nutrient-deficient eating or lack of exercise might not manifest immediate consequences, but over the years, the cumulative effect is considerable toxicity. Similarly, consistent neglect in relationships might, over time, erode the bonds of trust and intimacy, with emotional distances too challenging to bridge.

This duality underscores the energy opened in our choices and mindfulness. Every action, every decision, even however minute, is a step in a more extensive journey that can inspire us to be more deliberate. The awareness that today's habits are tomorrow's destiny can be a guiding beacon, urging us to invest in actions that align with our long-term visions and aspirations.

In this interconnected world, where immediate results often overshadow long-term gains, embracing the compounding effect requires patience, perseverance, and a deep-seated belief. It demands faith in the unseen, in the ripples that our actions create, which might not be evident immediately but will manifest in due course. This is a problematic area for many counselees. Generational wealth doesn't happen overnight, at least for most people.

The beauty of the compounding effect lies in its universality and its accessibility. It's a reminder that greatness isn't always born out of monumental leaps but often from tiny, consistent steps taken with conviction and purpose. It champions the idea that every individual, irrespective of their starting point, possesses the potential to shape their destiny, one action at a time. The compounding effect is a gentle yet powerful force, echoing the wisdom of ancient sages and the rhythms of nature. It's a call to appreciate the journey of transformation.

The Role of External Influences

Our environment, including our social circle, workplace, and cultural backdrop, is instrumental in our emotional transactions. Various external influences are transactional. Toxic environments constantly devalue, undermine, and increase the rate of emotional withdrawals. Constructive communities on the flip side, being part of a supportive community, can lead to consistent emotional deposits. The digital age and the omnipresence of social media mean that comparisons, criticisms, and validations are more accessible than ever. Navigating this digital landscape without affecting our emotional balance is a modern-day hurdle.

Embracing Fluidity

Identity, by its very nature, is fluid. As we evolve, our needs and aspirations change. Thus, the nature and frequency of our emotional transactions also shift. Embracing this fluidity, rather than resisting it, sustains a harmonious emotional balance. In the marketplace of life, our emotional transactions deliver substance in meaning and relevance. The transactions of deposits and withdrawals increase self-worth, confidence, and contentment when welcomed with awareness and intention.

As we distinguish the matured intricacies of our Identity ATM in the subsequent chapters, we will focus on harnessing our emotional wealth for a purposeful, joyful life. Remember, every transaction, no matter how insignificant it seems, shapes our identity's narrative. Being an active, conscious participant in this process shapes a legacy of emotional richness.

Questions for reflection:

1. When have I felt emotionally depleted after an interaction, and what was the underlying cause??
2. Can I recall a time when a conversation or experience filled me with positive energy?
3. How do I typically respond when faced with adversity? Do I retreat or seek support?
4. In what situations have I observed myself bouncing back stronger after an emotional setback? What internal or external factors aided my recovery?
5. How do past emotional transactions influence my present interactions? Any residual feelings or cloudy judgment?
6. Are there patterns in my emotional transactions that signal areas of personal growth or opportunities for resilience-building?
7. Can I identify individuals or experiences that have served as resilience role models? What lessons have I gleaned from observing or interacting with them?
8. How do I recharge and rejuvenate after a particularly taxing emotional transaction? Are there self-care routines or practices I can adopt to proliferate resilience?
9. How has resilience played a role in shaping my character, beliefs, and aspirations?

Identity Equity: Investing in a Richer Self

Chapter Concept: Identity equity benefits the positive impact we have investing in ourselves and others.

Chapter Strategy for Enrichment: Compare how building equity mitigates emotional and mental liabilities for diversification into other areas of our lives.

Emotional funds in our identity account stands out as a cornerstone in our ability to connect with our true identity. Like a shareholder investing in a company, every emotion, experience, and choice dispenses into the equity realm of our self-worth and confidence. Our emotional equity determines our resilience, perspective, and overall satisfaction as we move through life's various seasons.

The Concept of Emotional Equity

Emotional equity can be understood as the stored up feeling of self-worth accumulated over years of experiences, choices, and contemplation. It's not just about momentary feelings but a sustained belief in one's value, irrespective of external validations. At birth, we all possess an inherent value. This fundamental self-worth forms the initial capital of our emotional equity. Experiences either add to or detract from this equity. Achievements, positive affirmations, and growth experiences counter the detractions found in setbacks and criticisms. Just as investments yield dividends, our emotional equity provides consistent feelings of contentment, purpose, and belonging. The richer our emotional equity, the higher these dividends.

Our values act as the PIN to our Identity ATM. By reassessing and realigning these values, we can gain better control over our emotional transactions, securing a confident balance. When we open a bank account, setting a PIN is a requirement, so our funds are secure, and only we maintain that access. Our values protect us from life experiences and help us maintain access to the priorities of our lives. Values are steadfast lighthouses, guiding our journeys through calm and turbulent waters. They are the foundational beliefs that influence our perceptions, drive our actions, and ultimately shape our identities, which compete against the transactions we have in life. Yet, how these values are determined, prioritized, and protected, and how they inject into our emotional well-being, is akin to unraveling the threads that weave our lives together.

The origins of our values are steeped in a blend of personal experiences, cultural influences, familial teachings, and societal norms. We are subtly and overtly exposed to various beliefs and ideas from a young age. The stories we hear, the traditions we observe, and the behaviors we witness all leave indelible marks, gradually molding our value system. For instance, a child raised in a household that emphasizes community and collaboration might grow to value teamwork and unity. In contrast, one nourished in an environment of independence and exploration might prioritize self-reliance and curiosity.

As we journey through life, these values often undergo a prioritization process. Not all values hold equal weight at every stage of our lives. Personal experiences, both triumphant and challenging, play pivotal roles in this reshuffling. Someone who experiences betrayal might prioritize trust and loyalty in subsequent relationships. Conversely, individuals who find fulfillment in solitary pursuits might value introspection and solitude more.

Upholding these values becomes an ongoing endeavor, especially when confronted with conflicting external pressures. In a world of diverse beliefs and ever-shifting norms, staying true to one's values requires both introspection and fortitude. This is where setting boundaries, asserting one's beliefs, and consciously choosing environments and associations that resonate with our values becomes paramount. It determines resilience and a steadfast commitment to oneself, even in the face of opposition.

The correlation of values to our emotional well-being is fulfilling. When our actions and choices align with our core values, we experience a sense of harmony, purpose, and fulfillment. This alignment acts as an emotional buffer during challenging times and amplifies joy during moments of triumph. Conversely, when we drift away from our values or compromise them, it often results in emotional discord, manifesting as restlessness, dissatisfaction, or guilt.

Furthermore, our values become the lens through which we interpret the world around us. They influence our relationships, our aspirations, and our sense of self-worth. When our interactions and endeavors echo our values, they fortify our emotional well-being, creating a virtuous cycle of positive reinforcement. Therefore, individuals who prioritize their values often exhibit greater emotional resilience, adaptability, and contentment.

In essence, values are more than mere beliefs or ideals; they are the compass of our emotional landscape. They provide direction, clarity, and meaning to our existence. Values help us live life with purpose and conviction and respond with an inspirational environment where fulfillment, well-being, and unaltered joy can flourish.

Building and Nurturing Emotional Equity

Accumulating emotional equity is a continuous process. Let's explore the pathways to build or foster this invaluable asset. In a world where economic equity is frequently discussed, debated, and sought after, the concept of emotional equity is often overshadowed, albeit its significance remains undeniable. Emotional equity refers to the balance and fairness in emotional exchanges within and in our interactions with the world. Just as financial equity is a measure of justice in economic dealings, emotional equity speaks to the harmonious distribution of emotional experiences, ensuring that no aspect of our emotional life is undervalued or overburdened. It's about creating a sense of balance, a foundation from which we can draw strength, clarity, and purpose. As we notice more abundant ways to acquire emotional equity, it's essential to explore its nature, from self-awareness and emotional literacy to refining supportive environments and pursuing genuine connections.

At the heart of emotional equity lies the thorough comprehension of oneself. Self-awareness is often regarded as the first step towards emotional intelligence. We must first become astute observers of our emotional landscapes. This means pausing, reflecting, and being aware of the triggers of our emotional responses. By pointing out the patterns in our emotional reactions, we begin to discern which aspects of our lives might be receiving too much emotional energy and which might be starved recalibration based on insights results in a more balanced distribution of our emotional investments.

Emotional literacy further refines this journey. It's the ability to not only identify emotions but also to express them effectively and constructively. A robust emotional vocabulary empowers us to articulate our feelings, desires, and boundaries clearly. When we can communicate our emotional needs, the chances of misunderstandings and emotional imbalances diminish substantially. This form of literacy produces deeper connections, paving the way for enhanced emotional equity in interpersonal relationships.

While individual introspection and literacy are foundational, our environments play an equally pivotal role. Conceiving sacred spaces at home, work, or social settings that honor emotional expression and encourage open dialogue can significantly enhance emotional equity. In such spaces, every emotion, from the euphoric highs to the melancholic lows, finds a voice and an attentive ear. Such environments normalize emotional discussions and diminish the stigmas often associated with certain feelings, particularly those deemed harmful or vulnerable.

Emotional equity, however, isn't solely about the self and immediate environment. It extends to the broader realm of societal interactions and connections. Building genuine connections based on empathy, active listening, and mutual respect are more equitable emotional exchanges. Grounded relationships open a free flow of emotions, where neither party feels suppressed or overwhelmed. Such relationships become the bedrock of emotional support during tumultuous times and amplifying joy during moments of elation.

Another avenue to nurturing emotional equity is through intentional practices like mindfulness and meditation. These practices anchor us in the present, enabling a clearer perspective on our emotional state. Being present makes us more attuned to our emotional needs, and we can take proactive steps to address any imbalances. Over time, mindfulness yields a sense of inner calm and balance, fortifying our emotional reservoirs.

The narrative of emotional equity remains embedded within our quest for meaning and fulfillment. Like any form of equity, it requires vigilance, effort, and continuous recalibration. It asks us to be gentle, assertive, listen, express, and seek support. By consciously nurturing emotional equity, we embark on a transformative journey that promises personal growth and creates a world where emotions are celebrated, understood, and honored. Emotional equity is the harmonious symphony of our inner world, resonating with the melodies of balance and genuine connection. We not only enhance our own lives but also balance out the broader narrative of emotional wellness.

Protecting Emotional Equity

Accumulating emotional equity is half the battle; protecting it is equally worthy. In today's digital age, what we consume, be it news, social media, or entertainment, immensely affects our emotional state. Being mindful of this consumption is key. Regularly reviewing their portfolios and regular emotional check-ins help address potential liabilities. External perspectives from friends, mentors, or therapists deliver invaluable insights into our emotional well-being.

Our emotional needs evolve as we journey through life's various stages, from youth to old age. However, the constant through these seasons is the emotional equity we've accumulated. In the early stages, the pressing, initial objective is to build a strong foundation by seeking diverse experiences and forming positive beliefs. As responsibilities increase into adulthood, enhancing emotional equity through balanced relationships, self-care, and continuous learning becomes more influential. Prioritize your Identity ATM to reap the benefits of emotional equity, guaranteeing that the emotional investments made continue to pay off dividends.

Emotional equity, with its sagacious influence on our well-being, is an asset worth revering. It's the bedrock on which our self-worth, confidence, and resilience futures are built upon. We can have a secure and fulfilling emotional journey by being drawn to its significance, investing wisely, and defending it diligently. It also highlights the nature of equity, in that it is easy to grow more of it once you have equity. The Identity ATM's support function here is seeing how your self-esteem and confidence contribute to developing even more of it in yourself and others.

Emotional Liabilities

Emotional equity has often been touted as the touchstone for well-being and balance. However, just as in the financial world, where assets and equity are juxtaposed with liabilities, our emotional landscape is dotted with its share of liabilities. Emotional liabilities are those burdens, unresolved traumas, inhibitions, and internal conflicts that weigh us down, hindering our emotional growth and well-being. They act as anchors, often pulling us back into the past or tethering us to unproductive behavior and thought patterns. Addressing these emotional liabilities becomes central to our journey toward emotional freedom and maturity.

Emotional liabilities often find their origins in early life experiences. The tapestry of our childhood, woven with threads of interactions, observations, and experiences, leaves an indelible imprint on our emotional psyche. For many, this holds memories of love and care. However, interspersed might be patches of trauma, neglect, or misunderstanding. Such experiences manifest as emotional liabilities in our adult lives, especially when left unprocessed. They surface as trust issues in relationships, insecurities in our professional lives, or even as inexplicable bouts of anxiety or sadness.

Beyond childhood, as we tread the path of life, we inevitably encounter betrayals, failures, and rejections. Each of these, depending on our resilience and coping mechanisms, has the potential to add to our cache of emotional liabilities. A betrayal in a close relationship can lead to pervasive trust issues, a professional setback might birth debilitating self-doubt and societal rejections can sow seeds of identity crises.

Emotional liabilities are also linked with societal conditioning. The societal constructs of success and failure, of what's normal and different, affect our emotional liabilities. Constantly being measured against these often unrealistic and narrow benchmarks, individuals might grapple with feelings of inadequacy, low self-worth, or even existential dilemmas. The demands of societal expectations and the perpetual race to fit in suppresses emotions, desires, and identities, further adding to emotional liabilities.

However, one of the most insidious aspects of emotional liabilities is their tendency to beget more liabilities.

Individuals with unaddressed emotional burdens tend to adopt maladaptive coping mechanisms, such as substance abuse, avoidance, aggression, or perpetual victimhood. These mechanisms, dispensing momentary relief, compound the emotional distress in the long run. It's akin to a snowball effect, where unresolved emotional burdens gather more momentum as they roll down the slope of time.

Addressing emotional liabilities requires a multi-pronged approach. Firstly, self-awareness stands paramount. The journey towards addressing these liabilities begins with acknowledging their existence. It's about tuning in, listening to the whispers of our souls, and recognizing patterns in our emotional responses. Often, a recurring emotional pain point or trigger points towards an underlying liability.

The next step is seeking context and the accompanying origins of these liabilities. This might involve revisiting past traumas or experiences, a journey that can be painful but is essential for healing. The 'why' behind our emotional burdens helps contextualize them, making them less daunting and more manageable. Professional therapy can be instrumental in this journey. Professional therapists provide a non-judgmental, often sacred, space for individuals to unpack, dissect, and process their emotional liabilities. Their expertise guides the healing process with tools, insights, and perspectives backed by studies and evaluations.

Another potent tool in addressing emotional liabilities is cultivating mindfulness and emotional literacy. Being present, practicing mindfulness, and meditation can help individuals detach from overwhelming emotions, view them objectively, and address them without getting consumed. Conversely, emotional literacy equips individuals with the vocabulary and articulation to express their emotional burdens effectively.

While challenging, emotional liabilities are integral to the human experience. They shape our perspectives, behaviors, and interactions. However, they needn't define us. These liabilities can be addressed, transformed, and even leveraged for personal growth with awareness, support, and resilience. After all, shadows exist only when there's light, and the interplay of darkness and luminance adds depth and dimension to our journey. By addressing our emotional liabilities, we lighten our emotional load and pave the way for more affluent and fulfilling experiences.

Emotional Diversification

In financial investing, diversification is a strategy to spread investments across various assets to reduce risk. Similarly, emotional diversification involves investing in multiple experiences, relationships, and self-growth avenues toward a balanced emotional portfolio. Varied and diverse experiences, be it travel, learning new skills, or meeting different people, propel one to holistic emotional growth. Investing in balanced relationships with family, friends, mentors, and peers are multiple avenues for emotional support and development. Personal growth shouldn't be one-dimensional. Emotional, intellectual, spiritual, and physical growth avenues should all be pursued.

Emotional well-being and self-value are like the perennial rivers that carve their way through the landscapes of our lives. While they may seem self-sufficient, these rivers are fed by various tributaries. Primarily among them are our mental, spiritual, and physical growth. The synergy of these three realms cleverly influences our emotional equilibrium and shapes our intrinsic sense of worth.

Mental growth encompasses our cognitive abilities, critical thinking capacity, and quest for knowledge and validation. As we nourish our minds, exposing them to new ideas and experiences, we expand our horizons and bolster our emotional well-being. A mentally stimulated mind is often more resilient, better equipped to handle life's vicissitudes, and less prone to stagnation. We reinforce our self-esteem and self-worth whenever we conquer a new mountain, learn a new skill, or overcome a mental obstacle. This sense of accomplishment is an antidote to feelings of inadequacy or stagnation, fortifying our emotional foundation.

Moreover, a growth-oriented outlook enables us to view rough patches not as insurmountable hurdles but as opportunities to experience life in a new, much more positive way. Such a perspective transforms our emotional responses to setbacks, making us less susceptible to prolonged bouts of despondency or frustration. Instead, we become adept at extracting lessons from our experiences, further solidifying our emotional resilience and intrinsic value.

Spiritual growth enters the ethereal realm of our existence. Spiritual growth speaks to our connection with the universe, purpose, and innermost essence, regardless of religious beliefs. Spiritual practices, meditation, prayer, or simply contemplation nourish our souls. It serves as a sanctuary of peace, solace, and perspective during tumultuous times. As we evolve spiritually, we perceive ourselves as part of an interconnected cosmos, transcending the myopic view of self-centered existence. This cosmic perspective engenders feelings of belonging, reducing feelings of isolation or existential angst.

Furthermore, spiritual growth often matures the virtues of compassion, empathy, and gratitude. These virtues enhance our interpersonal relationships and amplify our emotional well-being. A heart filled with gratitude and compassion radiates positivity, elevating our mood and reinforcing our self-worth.

Lastly, physical growth and well-being, often the most tangible, are pivotal in shaping our emotional wellness. Our bodies are the tangible vessels of our existence, and their state influences our mental and emotional landscapes. Physical activities release a cocktail of endorphins, also known as nature's feel-good chemicals. These endorphins are natural mood lifters, combatting feelings of sadness, anxiety, or lethargy.

Physical growth goes beyond just fitness; it's also about nourishing our bodies with wholesome nutrition and adequate rest. A well-nourished and rested body is like a finely tuned instrument, resonating harmoniously with our mental and emotional states. The act of caring for our bodies, of investing time and effort in their well-being, also boosts our self-value. It sends a powerful message to our psyche about our worthiness and deservingness of care and love.

Moreover, as we witness the positive changes in our physique, stamina, or flexibility, our self-esteem gets a natural boost. The discipline and commitment required for physical growth translate into a heightened sense of accomplishment and self-worth.

In intertwining ways, the triad of mental, spiritual, and physical growth crafts a holistic framework for our emotional well-being and self-value. Each realm, while distinct, complements and amplifies the others, creating a harmonious symphony of holistic strength. Investing in our mental stimulation, spiritual exploration, and physical well-being fertilizes a fertile ground for robust emotional stability and an unwavering sense of self-worth.

With its ebbs and flows, life's journey is bolstered by the continuous pursuit of growth in these three dimensions. They are the pillars that support the edifice of our emotional well-being and state that regardless of external circumstances, our inner sanctum remains a haven of peace, positivity, and unwavering self-value. Embracing this holistic approach to growth transforms our perception of self and life experience, making them vibrant and meaningful experiences.

Building upon the triad of mental, spiritual, and physical growth, the interwoven nature of these realms is not a mere coincidence but instead reflects the design of human existence. Any single dimension doesn't capture our essence as beings; the amalgamation of our cognitive capacities, spiritual depths, and physical prowess truly defines us.

Recently, there's been a renewed emphasis on holistic well-being, a testament to the collective realization in each aspect of our existence. We live in an era of information overload, where our mental faculties are constantly engaged. While this continuous stimulation suggests unprecedented opportunities for intellectual growth, it also presents unique challenges. Mental fatigue, decision paralysis, and cognitive burnout have become prevalent, underscoring the need for deliberate mental nourishment and downtime. Undertaking mentally stimulating activities can be balanced with intentional periods of disengagement, such as meditation or nature observation, to rest and rejuvenate the mind.

Our spiritual well-being is confronted with the modern world's relentless pace and distractions. In the hustle and bustle of daily life, the whispers of our souls are often drowned out. However, setting aside time for spiritual introspection through religious practices, meditation, or silent contemplation can help reestablish that lost connection. These moments of spiritual immersion act as anchors amidst life's storms with a broader perspective of our existence.

Similarly, our physical well-being is under siege from sedentary lifestyles, processed foods, and erratic sleep patterns. However, the human body is remarkably adaptive and responsive. Even small, consistent efforts toward physical betterment, like daily walks, yoga, or adopting a balanced diet, can yield eminent benefits over time. As we witness our bodies respond, becoming fulfilled and more vibrant, it is a powerful reminder of our inherent capability for transformation and growth.

Two Must-Have Transactions for Your Healthy Transformation

Drinking water and sleeping are arguably two of the most critical components for maintaining mental clarity and emotional balance. The human body is an intricate machine that requires proper maintenance to function optimally, and these two activities are fundamental for its upkeep.

Water: The Essence of Life

Water is the essence of life and if science class from decades ago still holds true, it makes up about 60% of the human body and is involved in practically every aspect, from digestion and circulation to temperature regulation and cell health. When it comes to brain function, water is vital for producing neurotransmitters and hormones responsible for our thoughts and emotions. Even mild dehydration can impair attention, memory, and other cognitive functions.

A hydrated brain is a healthy brain. Water supports all brain functions, including thought and memory processes. When we drink water, we replenish the fluids lost through metabolism, breathing, sweating, and the removal of waste. It helps to keep the brain sufficiently hydrated to allow it to operate at peak capacity. Adequate water intake can sharpen our concentration, prevent and relieve headaches, and mitigate mood swings.

Moreover, water has a significant impact on stress levels. Dehydration increases the body's cortisol levels, which is the hormone associated with stress. Maintaining a good level of hydration can, therefore, reduce stress and promote calmness. It's not uncommon for people to report feeling more relaxed and clear-headed after drinking a glass of water.

Sleep: The Rejuvenating Force

On the other side of the spectrum, sleep is the rejuvenating force that allows our bodies and minds to rest and repair. Sleep is as vital to our health as food and water. During sleep, our bodies process information, consolidate memory, and regulate emotions. A good night's sleep can enhance learning, problem-solving skills, and creativity.

When we are asleep, our brain doesn't just shut down. Instead, it goes through several stages, each with its own purpose. For instance, the deep stages of sleep are crucial for consolidating memories and releasing hormones that regulate growth and appetite. Moreover, during REM (Rapid Eye Movement) sleep, our brain is almost as active as when we are awake. This stage of sleep is vital for processing emotions and solidifying memories.

Lack of sleep can immediately affect mood, leading to irritability and lack of focus. Chronic sleep deprivation increases risk to prolonged and severe mental health issues. Sleep affects our psychological state and can influence our perceptions and reactions. When well-rested, we are more likely to approach our problems with patience and clarity, making sleep essential for emotional resilience and mental health.

Synergistic Relationship

Drinking water and sleep have a synergistic relationship when it comes to cognitive function and emotional well-being. Dehydration can lead to tiredness, which in turn can negatively impact the quality of sleep. Similarly, poor sleep can lead to an imbalance in the body's regulation of fluids, potentially causing dehydration.

When we prioritize both hydration and sleep, we are setting up our bodies and minds for success. Proper hydration ensures that our physiological processes function correctly, promoting better sleep. A good night's sleep enables us to manage stress and maintain the motivation to make healthy choices, such as staying hydrated throughout the day. Keeping routines is the utmost factor. Regularly hydrate, monitor fluid loss with exertion, establish sleep routines, and maintain a restful environment when you do sleep.

Water and sleep are not just necessities but the foundations upon which our mental clarity and emotional stability rest. Both have profound effects on our cognitive functions and feelings, and by ensuring we get enough of each, we are taking significant steps towards a healthier, happier life. These two simple yet powerful aspects of our daily lives significantly influence the clearness of thought and emotional equilibrium we seek.

The journey toward holistic well-being is both an obstacle and a prospect. Each day presents a fresh canvas, an opportunity to paint a picture of tranquility, well-being, and longevity. By honoring each dimension of our existence with intention and care, we enhance our quality of life and deepen our relationship with the miracle that is human existence. While many things in your identity marketplace might be uncertain, your emotional equity's richness can be your guiding star, illuminating the path toward contentment and purpose.

Questions for Reflection:

1. What emotions do I most frequently experience, and how do they influence my interactions, decisions, and perceptions of the world around me?
2. In which situations or relationships do I feel most emotionally valued and understood, and why?
3. Can I identify any patterns or triggers of emotional depletion or strain in my life? How can I proactively address these to maintain emotional equilibrium?
4. How do my core beliefs and values align with the emotional exchanges and relationships? Are there any misalignments that need addressing regarding emotional equity?
5. In what ways do I actively invest in my emotional well-being or protect myself from consistently running on an emotional deficit?
6. How do I respond when emotional liabilities in my life, such as unresolved trauma, suppressed emotions, or negative self-talk, occur? What strategies can I employ to address and heal these areas?
7. What boundaries have been set or need to be placed around emotional well-being and emotional equity interactions with others?
8. How could you cultivate a supportive environment for relationships to champion mutual respect and still render investments into your emotional equity?

Identity Capital: Investing in Self-Esteem, Confidence and Connections

Chapter Concept: Emotional capital refers to the reserves of self-worth, resilience, and emotional strength we accumulate.

Chapter Strategy for Enrichment: Regular introspection, affirmations, and exposure to positive influences build emotional capital.

Occasionally, we shall face transaction errors and moments when guilt and shame become overwhelming. This chapter introduces coping mechanisms and strategies to overcome these setbacks so that our Identity ATM remains in good working order combined with the identity capital needed to function daily.

Investing in Self-Esteem

Self-esteem is often likened to the foundation of a building. Like a sturdy foundation with a structure's accompanying stability and longevity, satisfied self-esteem forms the bedrock of our psychological well-being. It shapes how we discover ourselves, interact with others, and screen against the forces shaking one's foundation. Unlike a building's foundation, which is laid once and then forgotten, self-esteem requires continuous repairs and reviving investments.

From the early days of childhood, several external factors start to influence our self-worth. Praise, criticism, comparison, successes, and failures all contribute to the developing narrative of how we view ourselves. Over time, this narrative can either empower us, making us resilient in the face of adversity, or it can become a debilitating force, casting shadows of doubt, insecurity, and inadequacy over our every move.

However, herein lies the beauty of self-esteem, it's dynamic. No matter our past experiences or beliefs about our worth, we have the agency to invest in and elevate our self-esteem. This journey begins with introspection. We can discern objective truths from distorted beliefs by delving deep into our psyche and the origins of our self-perceptions. This aids in reclaiming our intrinsic worth or, at a minimum, verifies the long-held beliefs needed to begin the journey toward auditing our Identity ATM accounts.

Once we have this clarity, the next phase involves challenging and reshaping negative or limiting beliefs.

For instance, if past failures have led us to believe we're inherently incapable, we must confront this narrative. By labeling failure as not a reflection of our worth but a natural part of growth and learning, we can disentangle our self-worth from external outcomes. This shift in perspective is transformative. It grapples with resilience and encourages the risk-taking and exploration components for personal growth and self-enhancement.

Concurrently, its secondary objective is to surround ourselves with positive influences. Just as a plant thrives in a conducive environment, our self-esteem blossoms when we affirm relationships and experiences. Trusting others who respect our worth, indulging in activities that amplify our strengths, and continuously seeking opportunities for self-improvement all facilitate building robust self-esteem.

Moreover, self-compassion serves a pivotal purpose. In our quest for perfection, we often become our harshest critics. While self-scrutiny is invaluable, it's equally gratifying to approach our flaws and mistakes with kindness. By extending the same compassion to ourselves that we would to a dear friend, we fortify our self-esteem against the corrosive effects of undue self-criticism and regret.

Another instrumental aspect of investing in self-esteem is setting boundaries. Our worth means abiding by what we will not tolerate. Establishing clear boundaries in personal relationships, professional settings, or even our internal dialogues is a testament to our self-respect. It signals that our well-being and self-worth are paramount to us and the world. Celebrating our achievements, no matter how big or small, bolsters self-esteem. In the hustle and bustle of life, we often downplay our successes, focusing instead on the next goal. However, taking a moment to revel in our accomplishments and embrace a positive self-image. It serves as a reminder of our capabilities, resilience, and worth.

Investing in self-esteem comes with introspection, resilience, and an unwavering commitment to our well-being. However, the rewards of this investment carry an esoteric aura about them. A robust self-esteem enhances our mental well-being, life experiences, and how we remember them, paving the way for fulfilling relationships, meaningful pursuits, and an abiding sense of contentment. In cherishing our intrinsic worth, we equip ourselves with the most potent tool to traverse life with grace, confidence, and joy.

Evolving Confidence: The Lifelong Endeavor

If one of many emotions consistently influences our actions, aspirations, and interactions, it would undoubtedly be confidence or lack thereof. More than just a fleeting feeling, confidence is an evolving construct, a force that has the power to shape our life's trajectory. Investing in this invaluable asset is, therefore, paramount.

When we think of confidence, we often visualize it as an innate trait, something one is born with or without. However, this perception couldn't be further from the truth. Confidence is the result of a multitude of experiences, internal exploration, and conscious choices. Every time we face our fears or even step out of our comfort zones, we deposit into our reservoir of confidence.

The early stages of developing confidence often hinge on external validations. A teacher's praise, a parent's encouragement, or even a friend's admiration can boost our self-belief as children. However, as we transition into adulthood, the sources of confidence evolve. It becomes less about external affirmations and more about internal convictions. This shift sustains confidence. By basing our self-belief on our abilities, values, and insights, we insulate it from external validations' erratic and often unpredictable nature.

Investing in confidence is a multifaceted endeavor. Firstly, it involves actively seeking out experiences that stretch our capabilities, with a push/pull effect on our competency and comfort. This might mean picking up a new skill, taking on leadership roles, or pursuing passions we've long shelved due to fear or doubt. Such experiences, even in failures, are invaluable. They expand our skill set and offer insights into our resilience, adaptability, and tenacity. Each endeavor, successful or not, adds a brick to the edifice of our confidence.

Simultaneously, mental and emotional well-being is intertwined with confidence. Caring for a positive self-image, practicing self-compassion, and managing anxieties and fears are pivotal in self-belief enhancements. This might involve professional counseling, meditation, or even simple practices like journaling or dedicating ourselves to affirming self-talk. Challenging self-limiting beliefs can catalyze a transformation in our confidence levels.

However, like any asset, confidence is vulnerable. It can be eroded by negative experiences, toxic relationships, or even our internal dialogues. Honing one's confidence involves setting boundaries, both with self and others. This means distancing ourselves from naysayers and detractors, not entertaining, self-deprecating thoughts, and not basing our self-worth on external success metrics or societal validations.

Imagine your accumulated self-belief, self-worth, and past achievements as funds deposited in the bank of your psyche. However, as with financial transactions, being wary of overdrawn accounts is essential. Continuously tapping into confidence without making corresponding deposits depletes our reserves. Hence, it's necessary to replenish this emotional currency. It's worth noting that sometimes, external factors might cause a temporary 'service outage' when we need to access our confidence account. Rejections, failures, or negative feedback can make accessing confidence challenging. Keeping in mind that temporary disruptions occur and focusing on steady "deposits," the reserves remain accessible.

In essence, managing confidence is strikingly similar to managing finances -balancing between withdrawals and deposits, being aware of proactive steps to replenish reserves when low. By visualizing confidence in this manner, a strategic and mindful approach to maintaining our emotional well-being, especially when life presents its myriad of difficulties, we are equipped to face them head-on.

One of the less discussed yet potent avenues for bolstering confidence is the art of reflection. We reinforce our belief in our capabilities by periodically looking back at our journey, achievements, learnings, and development. It serves as a reminder of what we've achieved and the adversities we've overcome, the fears we've conquered, and the growth we've undergone.

Another essential aspect of maintaining confidence is flexibility. Adapting, evolving, and shifting perspectives ensures our confidence is flexible and firm. Life is unpredictable, filled with ups and downs, successes, and setbacks. A relaxed confidence that can weather failures and adapt to new situations is far more sustainable. It's a confidence that says, "I might not have succeeded today, but I've learned, and I'll adapt."

Undeniably, confidence plays the role of both the thread and the needle. It forms the fabric of our experiences and guides our journey through the patterns of aspirations, joys, and setbacks. Confidence requires a commitment to ensuring that our journey through life is driven not by fears, doubts, or external validations but by an unwavering belief in our worth, capabilities, and potential. Living a life of purpose and joy is a promise to oneself to stay true to one's values, strive for meaningful goals, and find happiness in the journey.

Humility, Arrogance, and Confidence: The Delicate Balance

Among the multitude of identity expressions and character traits, humility, arrogance, and confidence often emerge as central figures, each influencing the other, determining our interactions, and molding our self-perception. The subtext of these attributes is that one must first applaud the notion they are not distinct, isolated entities. Instead, they often exist on a continuum, with their expressions influenced by internal beliefs and external situations.

Starting with confidence this trait is commonly understood as a belief in one's abilities, knowledge, and strengths. Rooted in self-assurance, confidence is empowering. It propels individuals to face risk head-on and persevere in adversity. When reinforced and grounded in actual capabilities and achievements, confidence is a beacon, illuminating paths and possibilities that might otherwise go unnoticed. Risky decisions highlight our need to connect to other pieces of information. Knowingly or unknowingly, business managers and military leaders are always assessing risk. How likely will something happen, what frequency will it occur, and to what degree is its impact? These questions are helpful in the context of one's decision-making as well.

The line separating confidence from its shadowy counterpart, arrogance, can be easily crossed. In stark contrast to the empowering nature of confidence, arrogance is characterized by an inflated sense of one's abilities to the extent of belittling or dismissing others. While confidence says, "I am capable," arrogance declares, "I am superior." This superiority alienates individuals, fosters resentment, and, ironically, clouds judgment, steering toward misguided decisions or actions. Arrogance lacks the desire to embed risk assessment and preventative measures in decision-making.

But where does humility fit into this equation? Humility is being grounded in strengths and weaknesses, often confused with self-deprecation. It confirms that while one might be skilled or knowledgeable in certain areas, there's always more to learn. Humility embraces the vastness of human experience and signifies one's position within it. When juxtaposed with confidence and arrogance, humility emerges as a moderating force. It tempers confidence, ensuring it doesn't spill over into arrogance. A humble individual can be confident in their abilities yet simultaneously recognize the contributions of others, the value of collaboration, and continuous learning. In many ways, humility and genuine confidence are natural allies. They coexist, reinforcing and complementing each other.

On the other hand, arrogance stands in stark contrast to humility. While humility listens, learns, and grows, arrogance assumes, dismisses, and stagnates. In its blinding self-importance, arrogance often misses the nuances, insights, and perspectives that humility, with its open-mindedness and receptiveness, can grasp.

However, the relationship between these traits isn't static. An individual's position between humility and arrogance can shift based on experiences, feedback, introspection, and personal growth. For instance, a person might drift towards arrogance after achieving a pivotal milestone. Still, with reflection, feedback, and a genuine desire for growth, they can recalibrate, anchoring themselves once more on the stable grounds of humility and natural confidence.

This interplay becomes particularly pronounced in leadership roles. A confident, humble leader can inspire collaboration and drive innovation. They applaud each team member's value, creating an environment where ideas are shared freely, and collective success is celebrated. Conversely, an arrogant leader, driven by a misguided sense of superiority, can stifle creativity, breed resentment, and hinder progress. The inability to coach others' strengths into results creates a toxic work environment where the focus shifts from collective growth to ego appeasement.

Humility, confidence, and arrogance shape personal relationships' interactions, bonds, and perceptions. A person who exudes confidence yet remains grounded in humility is often seen as approachable, genuine, and trustworthy. Their interactions are characterized by mutual respect and growth. On the flip side, arrogance, with its inherent dismissiveness and superiority, can strain relationships, creating rifts.

The relationship between humility, arrogance, and confidence is a deeply interwoven one to capitalize upon. While each trait, in isolation, has implications and manifestations, their interplay shapes an individual's interactions, decisions, and growth. Vouching for where one stands between humility and arrogance is a cause for personal and collective growth. After all, in the delicate balance of these traits lies the potential for innovation, collaboration, and genuine progress. It's a balance that demands introspection, openness, and a ratification of the boundless potential and diversity of human experience.

Healthy Connections Confirm Healthy Expressions

Like most expressions of our identity, they are often confirmed through associations with other people. This emphasizes connections being established and prioritized. The Identity ATM reminds us to remain entrusted with the ones we care about. In times of distress or uncertainty, having someone to turn to, be it a family member, friend, or partner, is one of the functions of the Identity ATM. These people remind us of our worth, offer fresh perspectives, or lend a listening ear.

In contrast, toxic or superficial connections can exacerbate feelings of loneliness, inadequacy, or distress. They might breed negativity, induce feelings of self-doubt, or plant seeds of mistrust and insecurity. The Identity ATM teaches how to reinforce or remove the wall, brick by brick, to protect the heart, solidifying the truth they were formative boundaries or insecure barriers.

Relationships, be they friendships, romantic partnerships, or familial bonds, often serve as mirrors. Stable connections often develop based on our strengths, passions, and fears. Through interactions, disagreements, and discussions with our close ones, we glean insights about ourselves and the world around us. These relationships, comforting us while out of our comfort zones, make us question our beliefs and urge us to evolve. Our personalities are forged, refined, and understood in the crucible of healthy connections. One of the most percipient human needs is the need to belong. Connections provide that sense of belonging.

Connections give us a place, a community, or a significant other where we feel seen, understood, and valued. This sense of belonging has profound implications for our self-esteem, confidence, and overall mental well-being. Science has proven that being connected with a community has significantly contributed to lowering stress, anxiety, and suicide rates.

The moments of pure joy, be it shared laughter over an inside joke, mutual excitement over shared interests, or the quiet contentment of a deep conversation, often arise from hope-filled connections. These moments, fleeting as they might be, enhance our overall life satisfaction, making our journeys richer and more fulfilling. Life is fraught with both roadblocks and avenues. In the face of adversities, healthy connections become our access to safe passage. They offer support, advice, or sometimes just the comfort of presence. Working together and sharing our problems with others can help us develop our ability to persist and find effective ways to deal with difficulties. Relationships hold a distinctive and influential place in the expansive narrative of our lives. They are the transactions that directly impact our emotional account, sometimes with monumental deposits and, at other times, with influential withdrawals. The interplay between relationships and our emotional wealth is about internally and externally fulfilling connections.

Relationships in Our Identity Ecosystem

Relationships form the very fabric of our existence. From the earliest bond we form with our caregivers to the diverse connections over our lifetime, each relationship leaves an indelible mark on our emotional landscape. Our earliest relationships, especially with primary caregivers, set the tone for our expectations, trust levels, and attachment styles in subsequent connections. Every friendship, romantic relationship, professional association, and casual interaction grows the view held of self and others. Relationships often act as mirrors, reflecting our strengths, insecurities, aspirations, and fears. Most people fail in this regard in assuming or owning the insecurities of others when they displace or project their shame outwardly. It requires a smooth emotional landscape, not one with many holes, to traverse someone else's destructive behavior.

Categories of Relationships and Their Impact

Diverse relationships affect our emotional wealth differently and influence our emotional ledger. Familial Bonds are often the foundational relationships, including those with parents, siblings, and extended family, that carry the responsibility of legacy, expectation, and deep-seated patterns while depositing unwavering support. Friendships, as voluntarily chosen bonds, hold a special place. They impart camaraderie and shared experiences. Over time, these bonds can either strengthen or wane based on their transactions. Romantic and intimate partnerships carry the potential for intimacy, growth, and vulnerability. They also come with their own set of joys and lessons. Professional Associations, from mentors to colleagues to educators and counselors, shape our work identity, confidence, and growth trajectory. They convey opportunities for collaboration, learning, and, sometimes, competition. Other acquaintances and casual Interactions, though fleeting, can sometimes leave lasting impressions, reminding us of the interconnectedness of humanity.

Every relationship involves a series of emotional transactions. Navigating these can determine their transformation into the longevity of the relationship. Trust is the foundation of any robust relationship. Insightful emotional deposits are derived from vulnerability and sharing our fears and aspirations. Effective communication, both in listening and expressions, ensures clarity and reduces misunderstandings of emotional harmony. Setting and respecting boundaries, no different than we do for ourselves internally, ensures that neither party feels overwhelmed nor disrespected, mitigating the risk to the emotional wealth of both individuals. Creating memories together adds richness to the relational bond. Every relationship faces conflicts. Addressing them constructively, without depleting emotional reserves, is crucial.

Emotional Overdrafts in Relationships

While relationships can be the biggest source of joy, they can also impede emotional withdrawals. Mismatched expectations, past baggage, toxic patterns, and growth divergence deliberate nuances to the relationships we have in life. When expectations aren't communicated or aligned, disappointment and emotional strain surely follow.

Mingling with someone who carries past baggage requires a delicate balance of empathy, boundaries, and self-awareness. Their past experiences, traumas, or unresolved emotions can inadvertently influence your interactions, causing confusion, triggers, or unintended emotional spillovers. To ensure these don't adversely impact you, it's essential to approach such situations with a clear strategy.

Remember always to have a willing and open heart. Everyone has a history of experiences advancing and challenging the Identity ATM, contextualizing their reactions or behaviors. Someone's guarded nature or occasional outburst may be rooted in past events that have left an indelible mark on their psyche. Patience and an open mind can go a long way in bridging potential emotional gaps. It's not about responding to their baggage, per se, but acknowledging its presence as a gesture of empathy.

However, while empathy is a noble virtue, self-preservation may be equally nefarious. Establishing clear boundaries ensures you don't become an unintended recipient of their unresolved emotions. Communicate your limits assertively and consistently. This doesn't mean shutting them out but setting guidelines for all interactions. For instance, while you might be willing to listen, clarifying that certain behaviors or emotional outbursts directed toward you are unacceptable is essential.

Equal prominence should be found in the process of self-examination. Analyze your feelings and reactions post-interaction. If you find yourself disproportionately affected or emotionally drained, it might be worth reconsidering the potency of your relationship. Engaging with someone with past baggage should not consistently come at the cost of your emotional well-being.

Encouraging professional intervention can be beneficial. Although friends, family, or colleagues are normally part of one's trusted support system, sometimes professional expertise is necessary to deal with their complex issues. Encouraging someone to seek therapy or counseling can be a step towards healing for them.

Remember the significance of self-care. Intense emotions or past traumas can be taxing. Ensure you have avenues to recharge through personal hobbies, meditation, or simply spending time with loved ones who uplift you. Remember patience, empathy, and self-awareness for those who desire to project or displace their baggage onto you. While it's commendable to show support, it's equally central to ensure your emotional well-being remains uncompromised. By striking this balance, meaningful interactions are entrenched, irrespective of the shadows of the past. You may very well be a source of income into their Identity ATM while they are someone who withdraws from yours.

The High Cost of Toxic Relationships on Emotional Well-being

Toxic relationships, whether familial, romantic, or platonic, act as consistent drains on our emotional reserves, analogous to unauthorized withdrawals from a bank account. These relationships often manifest in manipulation, deceit, belittlement, and disregard for boundaries. Over time, the consistent negativity can deplete our emotional resources, leaving us feeling bankrupt and devoid of vitality.

Every instance of belittling, undermining, or invalidating comments made by a toxic partner or friend is akin to a withdrawal from our emotional savings. Instead of feeling valued and uplifted after interactions, we often find our self-worth diminished, questioning our decisions and doubting our intrinsic value. The constant need for approval, the perpetual walking on eggshells, and the continuous cycle of appeasement can act as recurring debits, drawing down our self-esteem, confidence, and joy reserves.

Furthermore, the unpredictability inherent in many toxic relationships oscillating between periods of love bombing and devaluation creates emotional volatility. This inconsistency can further tax our emotional bandwidth as we brace for the next outburst or conflict. Chronic stress, anxiety, and even physical repercussions exemplify the perpetual state of alertness and anticipation if unchecked. Much like financial insolvency can limit opportunities and possibilities in the material world, being emotionally drained also constrains our ability to remain captivated with life. The constant depletion can hinder our capacity to form relationships, pursue aspirations, or enjoy simple pleasures.

While every relationship has its ups and downs, toxic relationships result in a net loss, steadily eroding the richness of our emotional well-being. Proactively safeguarding our emotional capital is essential for maintaining long-term happiness. Relationships that involve manipulation, excessive criticism, or any form of abuse anchor chronic emotional depletion.

The Detriment of Growth Divergence on Emotional Reserves

Growth divergence where our actual personal development deviates from our desired or expected trajectory acts as a silent usurper of our emotional assets. Discord siphons our self-esteem and confidence with stealthy proficiency when we are lagging in personal, professional, or social spheres, especially compared to peers or personal benchmarks. Sometimes, individuals grow at different paces or in different directions. The result is emotional and value misalignment.

Such divergence can be particularly corrosive because it triggers a cascade of self-doubt. The inherent human tendency to compare and societal pressures to meet certain milestones by specific ages intensify feelings of inadequacy. Every observed shortfall, whether a career setback, delay in acquiring particular skills, or unmet personal goals, acts like a transactional fee, gradually diminishing our emotional savings.

These emotional deductions then prime us for feelings of guilt. In the quiet confines of introspection, questions like "Where did I go wrong?" or "Why am I not where I thought I'd be?" loom large. This guilt, often displaced, compounds the emotional deficit. We often blame ourselves for diverging paths rather than seeing individual growth journeys as unique.

The vulnerability created by this underachievement can further open the floodgates to external criticism or unsolicited advice, deepening feelings of ineptitude. It can be a vicious cycle: the more we feel we've deviated from our growth path, the more susceptible we become to guilt, and the more our self-worth erodes.

Additionally, growth divergence in relationships, particularly when one individual realizes themselves as advancing more than their counterpart, can introduce a collection of emotional challenges, maybe even volatility and instability. The individual progressing might inadvertently develop impatience, superiority, or frustration, while their partner may grapple with inadequacy, envy, or a diminishing sense of self-worth. This imbalance, if unchecked, can create an emotional chasm between the two, such as with the expressions of resentment and distance. The essence of a bond via shared experiences, mutual respect, and emotional reciprocity becomes strained as the divergent paths forge unaligned priorities, values, and aspirations. Over time, this can jeopardize the very foundation of the relationship, requiring proactive communication and empathy to bridge the growing divide. In essence, growth divergence doesn't just result in the benign surmise of unmet goals but rather in the active withdrawals from our emotional wealth. To safeguard our well-being, we must recalibrate our growth, appreciate the nonlinear nature of personal journeys, and avoid the pitfalls of unfavorable comparisons.

The Multifaceted Dimensions of Building Lasting Connections

The abstract architecture of long-lasting relationships is adorned by emotions and experiences, like two individuals living harmoniously. One foundational pillar of this bond is investing in quality time. Amidst the cacophony of the digital age, where screens often usurp faces and notifications overshadow conversations, carving out moments of genuine, uninterrupted connection becomes paramount. During these interludes, where the world's distractions fade into the periphery, two people can genuinely dive deep, exploring the caverns of each other's minds, emotions, and aspirations. Such moments bridge physical proximity and meld emotional landscapes, cementing the connection in shared experiences.

However, the mere presence isn't enough to propel intimacy; the depth of conversation acts as its lifeblood. Open dialogues, characterized by candid exchanges about feelings, hopes, fears, and dreams, sustain the relationship. Genuine connection is possible when two people can openly share their vulnerabilities, express their concerns, and communicate their expectations without fear. This level of transparency acts as a compass, steering the relationship through storms and tempests of doubts, anchoring it firmly on the shores of trust and mutual respect.

Yet, as we journey through life, we are ceaselessly molded by our experiences, constantly evolving our perceptions, beliefs, and personalities. Confronting this dynamism within ourselves and our partners is essential for the relationship's longevity. Continuous learning isn't just about external knowledge; it's about the ever-unfolding exploration of each other. Adaptability is born by embracing the reality that both individuals in the union are in flux. We learn to dance with the changes, accommodating new rhythms and beats, ensuring the relationship remains resilient against the trials of time.

Empathy emerges as a pivotal player amidst human connections. To move beyond acquaintance with another, feel their joys as your own, resonate with their sorrows, and take on a deliberate practice of empathy. When we endeavor to step into our partner's shoes, to view the world from behind their eyes, and to experience life from their vantage point, we build bridges of enlightenment. This empathetic lens often dissolves potential conflicts at their nascent stage and ignites a climate where disagreements mature into discussions rather than escalating into disputes.

However, amidst the conversations, there's a luminous thread of joy that should never be overlooked: the act of celebrating each other. Every milestone achieved, whether colossal or minuscule, deserves mentioning. We infuse the relationship with positive energy by rejoicing our partner's successes and being their most ardent cheerleader. These celebrations become deposits in the emotional account of the union, fortifying its foundation against potential tremors of doubt or insecurity.

In essence, the longevity of a relationship isn't governed solely by grand gestures or monumental declarations of love. Instead, the small, consistent actions—like spending undistracted time together, broadening the aperture of open dialogues, continuously learning about each other, practicing empathy, and celebrating every facet of each other—weave together to create an enduring bond. In this compelling mosaic of shared moments, emotions, and experiences, two souls find a harmonious rhythm, building a legacy of love that stands resilient against the sands of time.

The Journey of Solo Growth: Relationships with Self

In a world teeming with interconnections and networks of relationships, there lies a bond that often goes unnoticed, undervalued, and sometimes even neglected. In its innate significance, this bond stands paramount among all other relationships we kindle in our hearts. Working within the framework of the Identity ATM, the most important relationship is the one we have with ourselves. Like the roots of an ancient tree that anchor it deep within the earth, our relationship with ourselves forms the bedrock upon which the entire edifice of our external connections stands. To truly synchronize the essence of our innermost bond, we must comprehend its intentions, components, and impact on our life narrative.

The journey to a healthy relationship with oneself often commences with the art of inner contemplation. This isn't merely passive; it's active in the deepest recesses of our psyche. By regularly diving into the waters of introspection, we begin to chart the landscapes of our mind, our most innate needs, desires, strengths, and areas ripe for growth. This isn't just an academic exercise; it is a compass that guides our actions, decisions, and responses to life's obstacles. As we decipher the contours of our inner world, we equip ourselves by gaining knowledge to interact with the external world with grace and agility.

Merely comprehending something is just the beginning. We need to put in much effort to maintain our inner sanctum. This is where the role of self-care becomes indispensable. In a world that constantly vies for our attention, where the cacophony of responsibilities, aspirations, and societal expectations often drowns the whispers of our own needs, setting aside time for activities that rejuvenate our mind, body, and soul becomes not just essential, but sacred. Whether it's a solitary walk amidst nature, delving into the pages of a book, practicing meditation, or simply basking in the serenity of solitude, these acts of self-care are decorative to our emotional well-being.

Self-care carves a new path; establishing personal boundaries erects the walls that guard our sanctum. Like a unique piece of art, every individual has their emotional texture, limits, and thresholds. These limits testify to our self-awareness, but ensuring they're respected by ourselves and others is a testament to our self-respect. Boundaries aren't barriers; they delineate our personal space, ensuring our emotional, mental, and physical well-being remains inviolate.

In growing a harmonious relationship with oneself, affirmation and gratitude emerge as potent allies. Whispering words of self-affirmation isn't mere self-talk; it's a dialogue with our soul, a gentle reminder of our worth, capabilities, and potential. Coupled with gratitude, appreciating life's blessings nurtures positivity. This outlook, rooted in positivity, acts as a beacon, illuminating even the darkest corners of self-doubt on the path to becoming a robust and radiant relationship with ourselves.

In the theater of life, where we play countless roles and forge innumerable bonds, the relationship with oneself remains perhaps the most mysterious. It's the expression of our true essence, the anchor that grounds us in storms, and the compass that guides our voyage. By investing in this relationship, caring, establishing boundaries, affirming, and expressing gratitude, we don't just enrich our own lives; we elevate the quality of every external connection we form. For in the radiant glow of self-love and accompanying patience, we find the luminescence that lights up every path we tread and every bond we forge.

Relationships, with their ability to shape the collage of emotions, demand attention. The patterns and intricacies of relational transactions help shepherd connections that prosper, empower, and inspire.

In the subsequent chapters, we'll delve deeper into actionable tools to strengthen your relational vitality. As we traverse this journey, always remember that in life's grand narrative, relationships are the chapters that give our story depth, color, and meaning. Ensuring they add richness to our emotional wealth is both an art and a science we can all master with intention and effort. You need capital if you are going to invest. This applies to all types of investing, not just financially. Building capital in who you know yourself to be, with healthy balances of self-esteem and confidence, allows you to draw upon them when you are faced with conflict and difficult situations that would require your time, attention, and maturity.

Questions for Reflection:

1. In moments of introspection, what core values and beliefs consistently surface as pillars of your identity?
2. How do you measure the returns on your emotional investments within yourself and in relationships with others?
3. Which activities or practices do you find most rejuvenating to your emotional well-being?
4. Are there patterns in your reactions or behaviors that may signal unresolved emotional challenges?
5. How do you differentiate between relationships that spend your emotional capital wisely versus those that deplete it?
6. What strategies do you employ to bounce back from emotional setbacks, ensuring the preservation and growth of your emotional capital?
7. How do you cultivate a culture of open communication, ensuring that emotional needs and boundaries are clearly understood and respected?
8. How do you actively invest in deepening the association of your emotional needs with the people in your life?
9. How do you celebrate and acknowledge emotional growth and milestones in your relationship with yourself and others?

The Power of Personal Narratives: Crafting a Story of Strength and Resilience

Chapter Concept: We all have stories we tell ourselves, which shape our self-perception and life choices.

Chapter Strategy for Enrichment: Crafting a positive and empowering narrative can transform our lives.

Every individual's life is an unfolding story through the transactions with events, emotions, and decisions. Personal narratives are thus crucial in shaping our perceptions, behaviors, and overall emotional well-being in response to them. Based on healthy mental processing and insights, narratives craft a story that speaks truth to those transactions.

Listening to our feelings and thoughts is a profound exercise in self-awareness, a process that enables us to understand our innermost inclinations and responses to the world around us. Through this introspective listening, we gain insight into who we are, what we need, and what we value. This internal dialogue is not mere chatter but a guidepost to our emotional and mental well-being.

Feelings are often the most immediate signifiers of our internal state. They act as indicators, much like the lights on the dashboard of a car, signaling when something within us needs attention. Emotions such as joy, sadness, anger, and fear are not random; they arise for reasons, often in response to our interactions with others or to events in our lives. They can tell us about the things that matter to us, our boundaries, and the aspects of our lives that we may want to change. When we feel joy, it may be a sign that we are engaging in activities that align with our deeper passions. Conversely, persistent sadness or dissatisfaction might reveal a disconnect between our current situation and our aspirations or needs.

Similarly, our thoughts provide a continuous narrative that can shape our perception of ourselves and our environment. They can be reflective of deeply held beliefs and attitudes, some of which may be limiting or outdated. By examining our thought patterns, we can identify which of these serve us well and which may need to be re-evaluated or challenged. For example, a recurring thought that undermines our confidence could be rooted in an experience that no longer reflects our current reality or capabilities.

To listen effectively to our feelings and thoughts, we must cultivate a sense of mindfulness with a state of being present and fully engaged with the now without being overly reactive or overwhelmed by what's going on around us. It requires us to slow down, pay attention, and observe without immediate judgment or action. This deliberate pause provides the space necessary to recognize the message behind the emotion or thought.

Engage in practices facilitating inner communication. These activities encourage slowing down the mind and quieting the external noise, allowing us to hear our internal voice more clearly. Through meditation, we can observe our thoughts and feelings as they arise, noting them with detachment and curiosity. On the other hand, as previously mentioned, journaling can help us articulate these internal experiences, giving us a clearer picture of our mental and emotional patterns over time.

It is also important to recognize that not all thoughts and feelings are literal truths. They can be influenced by fatigue, hunger, stress, or external pressures, distorting their message. Therefore, part of listening to ourselves is discerning which feelings and thoughts are momentary and circumstantial and which are more deeply rooted and significant. This discernment allows us to respond appropriately, whether it's by addressing an immediate need or by engaging in deeper self-reflection and possibly seeking the support of others.

Listening to our feelings and thoughts is not always comfortable. It can bring to light insecurities, fears, and unresolved conflicts. However, it is through facing these uncomfortable truths that growth occurs. We can begin to work through issues, identify solutions, or make necessary changes in our lives. This self-knowledge empowers us to make choices that are in better alignment with our true selves, leading to a more authentic and fulfilling life.

Ultimately, our feelings and thoughts are a rich source of personal wisdom. They are the language of our subconscious, speaking to us of our needs, our dreams, and sometimes our deepest wounds. By learning to listen to what our inner experiences are trying to tell us, we open the door to deeper understanding and more intentional living. It is a process of continual learning, where each layer of understanding lays the foundation for the next. Through this ongoing conversation with ourselves, we can navigate life with greater confidence and clarity, armed with the knowledge of our innermost selves.

Personal Narratives

The personal narrative one crafts is a powerful tool that shapes every aspect of life. It governs how one approaches and interacts with self and others. While these stories are intrinsic to our identity, they are not set in stone. They evolve, shift, and metamorphose based on the influences and experiences that punctuate our existence.

From our earliest memories, our brains begin to absorb the environment around us. These formative years resemble the fertile soil where seeds of beliefs, perceptions, and self-worth are sown. The environment in which a child grows, the interactions they observe, and the feelings they internalize become the first chapters of their life story. A loving embrace can instill feelings of safety and belonging, while a harsh word can imprint an indelible mark of insecurity. The memories we accumulate during our younger years, both pleasant and traumatic, serve as a backdrop against which our future experiences are juxtaposed.

However, as one travels their respective life path, the story begins to expand its horizons, embracing influences from the broader world. Societal norms, cultural mores, and collective narratives enhance our story. The expectations of a community gathering are writing chapters to our ever-evolving tale. The values endorsed by our culture, the ideologies it upholds, and the ideals it venerates become the yardstick against which we measure our aspirations and dreams.

Yet, personal narratives are not solely products of external factors. One's journey is also molded through the landscape of success and failure. Every achievement, monumental or minute, adds a shimmering star to the sky of one's self-belief. It whispers words of encouragement, bolstering the spirit to aim higher and reach farther. On the other hand, failures, those inevitable companions on the journey of life, have the potential to darken the narrative. Unprocessed failures can cast long shadows of doubt, shrinking horizons and dimming aspirations. However, if viewed through the lens of learning, these setbacks can become stepping stones to extraordinary acumen and growth.

Intertwined with these personal highs and lows is the perpetual stream of feedback from the world. Every individual, knowingly or unknowingly, plays the part of a mirror, reflecting perceptions, beliefs, and feelings. The praise from a cherished mentor can kindle flames of passion and drive, motivating one to venture beyond familiar territories. Simultaneously, criticism can be a double-edged sword, especially from those we hold in high regard. While constructive feedback reinforces improvement and introspection, harsh or unjust criticism can dent the armor of self-worth.

In this grand narrative, it becomes integral to pause occasionally and listen. Listen to the stories we tell ourselves, sift through the chapters, and discern the themes that resonate most. It's essential to be the author of one's tale, hold the quill firmly, and ensure the narrative remains true to one's core. We can rewrite, edit, and sometimes even start afresh, creating a record that empowers, uplifts, and enlightens. The task of shaping our identity's narrative is a lifelong endeavor, constantly requiring updates, no different than smartphones needing software updates.

The Dual Nature of Narratives

Personal narratives can be empowering or limiting. While empowering narratives instill confidence, resilience, and positivity, limiting narratives can trap individuals in cycles of self-doubt, fear, and stagnation. Empowering narratives highlight strength, adaptability, growth, and potential. Limiting narratives focus on inadequacies, past failures, and external validations. They often include avoidance behaviors, fear of taking risks, and a constant need for external validation.

The stories we hold within ourselves, the ones we replay in our minds, possess immense power over our emotional landscape and ultimately shape our life's trajectory. These internal narratives, woven from memories, experiences, and societal influences, can either serve as anchors, grounding us in empowerment or chains, shackling us to a world of limitation and doubt.

At the heart of these stories lies self-esteem, which can be visualized as the lens through which we detect ourselves and our capabilities. When our internal narrative resounds with affirmations of worth, capability, and potential, it casts a radiant glow upon our self-image. This positive narrative becomes the bedrock of robust self-esteem. Each chapter of success, love, and kindness further embellishes this narrative, solidifying our belief in our intrinsic worth. Such individuals overtake life's ebbs and flows gracefully, acknowledging their value beyond fleeting circumstances. However, in stark contrast, a limiting narrative resonates with discordant notes of unworthiness, doubt, and inadequacy. It distorts the self-image, often clouding the myriad of strengths, talents, and potentials one possesses. Such a narrative can reduce the grand symphony of life to a few dissonant chords, diminishing self-esteem and casting shadows of doubt.

Yet, the impact of our internalized stories extends beyond our self-perception. They shape our approach to one of life's most vigorous terrains: decision-making. Every crossroad, every choice becomes a stage where our narrative either empowers or inhibits. Individuals with empowering narratives view the world as a canvas of possibilities. They are more inclined to venture into the unknown, take calculated risks, and passionately chase after their desires. The trust in their story emboldens them to make decisions that resonate with their heart's deepest longings. They discern opportunities even in adversities and are not easily deterred by setbacks. On the other end of the spectrum, those with limiting narratives often stand at life's crossroads with trepidation. Fear, doubt, and apprehension cloud their judgment, causing them to shy away from potential opportunities. Their choices are not so much driven by ambition as by an overwhelming desire to evade threats. Indecision or regrettable compromises mark the true nature of the narrative presented.

Furthermore, the tendrils of our internal stories extend into the realm of our interpersonal activity. The narratives we uphold become the scripts of our relationships. A buoyant tale celebrating love, trust, and familiarity naturally paves the way for honest, fulfilling relationships. Such narratives link genuine connections, mutual respect, and boundaries. They allow love to flourish without the shackles of insecurity or possession. Conversely, limiting narratives, especially those punctuated by past traumas or fears, often manifest in relationships as dependencies, insecurities, or even a perennial fear of abandonment. They can trap individuals in cycles of co-dependency, where the relationship becomes less about mutual growth and more about filling voids.

One of the most impactful of our internal narratives is evident in our resilience. When faced with life's storms, an empowering narrative serves as a sturdy ship, weathering the rough seas with determination and hope. These stories underscore the belief that obstructions are transient and that one possesses the strength to overcome and learn. Such narratives become wellsprings of hope, ensuring that the ember of optimism remains alight even in moments of despair. In contrast, a limiting narrative can be likened to a fragile vessel, easily overwhelmed by life's tumultuous waves. Such stories amplify feelings of despair as insurmountable mountains rather than gateways and options.

The stories we etch within our souls hold the power to either elevate or diminish our existence. They directly sculpt our emotional states, influence our behaviors, and determine our overall life satisfaction. However, the burdens of these narratives can eventually be transformative when transmitted via the Identity ATM. With empowering narratives, we can reframe our relationship with ourselves, others, and the world to a life brimming with purpose, joy, and fulfillment.

Re-writing the Narrative: Crafting an Empowering Story

Recognizing the power of personal narratives, it's essential to craft a story that serves our highest good actively. Use the following breakdown of a narrative to establish your own. After you review each step, read the two personal narratives as an example for you.

1. Awareness: The first step is increasing mindfulness within our current narrative. Journaling, introspection, or therapy can assist in this process.

2. Questioning Limiting Beliefs: Is the belief based on fact or assumption? Is it rooted in an experience that no longer holds relevance?
3. Affirmations: Use positive affirmations to reinforce empowering beliefs. Repeated affirmations can slowly change deeply entrenched narratives.
4. Visualizing Success: Visualization exercises can help in re-imagining one's story. Envisioning success, happiness, and fulfillment can slowly shift the narrative toward positivity.
5. Seeking Feedback: Sometimes, external perspectives may propose valuable insights and a trusted, objective feedback on one's self-perception.
6. Continuous Learning: Engaging in new experiences, learning new skills, and pushing boundaries is evidence against limiting beliefs and fuels a positive narrative.

Transforming Narratives

To illustrate the power of personal narratives, let's consider two real-life examples:

1.   Growing up in a critical household, Anna's narrative was one of inadequacy. Despite her achievements, she constantly felt like an impostor. Confessing the limiting nature of her story, she went to therapy, journaled, and sought mentorship. Over time, she shifted her narrative, focusing on her strengths, achievements, and potential. Today, Anna is a confident professional, mentoring others to find their voice.

2.   Raj's narrative was one of perpetual victimhood, stemming from his early life. He often felt the world was against him. After a personal setback, he

sought therapy, where he learned to reframe his experiences, focusing on lessons and growth. Raj's new narrative is one of resilience and strength. He now conducts workshops on resilience and personal growth.

Your Story

Your personal narrative holds immense power. They can either be chains that bind or wings that let us soar. Actively shaping our stories is an act of self-love and a journey toward true empowerment and fulfillment. And it is expected to have a narrative rooted in where you bank. For example, when your Identity ATM is banking with faith, the narrative may drive everything about the expression of your identity. The tenets of your faith may very well tell the narrative. Christians, for example, express they were a sinner but are now saved by grace and live a disciple of Christ way. The narrative becomes an expression of their identity as either sinner or saint. The emphasis begins with that awareness of your narrative and how it is formed and determines your access to the value it yields.

In the remaining chapters, we will dive deeper into tools, techniques, and practices that can assist in this transformative journey. Remember, while we might not have control over every event in our lives, we certainly possess the power to choose the story we tell about it. And in this story, you are the protagonist, deserving of love, growth, and every success.

Questions for Reflection:

1. What past experiences might have shaped my current limiting beliefs, and how can I reframe these experiences to absorb them in a new light?
2. Which of my beliefs might not truly be my own but have been instilled by societal norms, culture, or external pressures, and how can I start challenging these beliefs to align more with my values?
3. How can I craft powerful affirmations that counteract my limiting beliefs and resonate deeply with my aspirations, values, and authentic self?
4. When I visualize my most successful and fulfilled self, what does that look like regarding my career, relationships, and personal growth, and how can this vision guide my actions and decisions moving forward?
5. From whom should I actively seek feedback to ensure I'm not only reinforcing my strengths but also addressing growth areas, and how can I approach this feedback with an open heart and mind?

Joint Accounts in the Identity ATM

Chapter Concept: The Identity ATM represents an individual's sense of self, but the joint accounts of marriage and parenting present challenges to the balance.

Chapter Strategy for Enrichment: Assess the Identity ATM's requirements to reflect your individual identity when there are shared accounts to consider.

Understanding one's identity balance in marriage and parenting is akin to walking a tightrope where the roles of spouse and parent on either side must be navigated with careful precision to avoid losing one's sense of self. Identity is not static; it's dynamic, shaped by experiences, relationships, and responsibilities. The entrance into marriage and parenting introduces a profound shift in identity, demanding a recalibration of who we are, or think we are, and who we aim to become. Regarding the

Identity ATM, this is like having joint accounts with a significant other. There is complete access but without full control.

The endeavor begins with self-assessment. This is a deep, introspective journey into understanding what we value about ourselves, our unique attributes, and how these features have evolved. The transition into marriage often brings the challenge of blending personal identity with the shared identity of the partnership. Compromise becomes a currency of this new realm, where the value of sacrifice is often directly proportional to the relationship's health. Struggles in marriage are easily identified with the Identity ATM as it highlights one spouse depositing more into the account than the other. Though there will be times when one person may need to be the breadwinner financially, the confidence of the marriage should be upheld with deposits by both parties.

In the same breath, parenting adds a layer of complexity. It can simultaneously enrich and obscure personal identity, as the roles of caregiver, provider, and protector often take precedence over individual pursuits. This is where the understanding of identity balance becomes crucial. The balance isn't just about equal distribution of time or energy but an equilibrium where these demanding roles don't overshadow the essence of one's being. You are handing your children your worldviews, but at the same time, you must keep the change associated with the world they are growing up in.

Although your identity receives deposits and makes withdrawals in the marriage and parenting relationships, the transactions are transforming each of you individually as much as they are as a collective unit. Communication is the cornerstone of maintaining this balance. It involves expressing needs, desires, and boundaries to one's spouse. It is also about listening and understanding their perspective, creating that symbiotic relationship where both parties grow individually and together. It's the openness to share dreams and fears, building a foundation where the marriage survives and thrives on each person's uniqueness.

Marriage and parenting often require that parts of one's identity take a backseat to familial obligations. However, it's crucial to identify which parts of the self are non-negotiable, the core elements that make you who you are. Without this clarity, the risk of identity diffusion looms large, where one's sense of self is diluted to the point of invisibility.

Navigating this terrain also calls for an acknowledgment of harmony and conflict. Harmony arises when family life and personal identity complement each other. Conflict, while often viewed negatively, can be a catalyst for growth and a signal that aspects of one's identity need attention and nurturing. It's essential to recognize that sometimes, the most harmonious marriages and well-adjusted parenting styles are born out of resolving these conflicts in ways that honor individual identity.

Support systems play an integral role in maintaining identity balance. It's about creating space for personal development through friendships, hobbies, and self-care practices that fuel individuality. These systems serve as a reminder that while one may be a spouse and parent, they are also more than those roles.

A joint account -joint identity - with one's spouse can be enriching. It signifies weaving two threads to create a more robust, vibrant tapestry. Yet, within this interwoven piece, the individual threads remain distinct, contributing their unique color and texture to the overall design. This joint identity thrives on mutual respect for each person's uniqueness and a shared vision for the partnership.

Effort management emerges as a critical skill in this quest for balance. It's about creating pockets of time dedicated to personal growth and fulfillment, away from the responsibilities of marriage and parenting. Whether spent in solitude or pursuing individual passions, these moments recharge the spirit and affirm personal identity. The balance of identity in marriage and parenting is a delicate art. It requires constant vigilance and adjustment, an openness to growth, and a commitment to self-awareness. With these practices, individuals can maintain their unique essence while embracing the transformative experiences of marriage and parenting. This balance is beneficial for personal well-being and the cornerstone of healthy, resilient, and thriving family relationships.

Parenting philosophies and practices should ideally reflect one's core values so that parenting feels like an extension, rather than a suppression, of oneself. It's about imprinting one's values onto the next generation authentically without projecting their guilt and shame at the same time. Adaptation is inherent to this journey for everyone involved. As individuals and relationships mature, so should the understanding and expression of identity. Accepting that change is integral to life's cycle is vital to maintaining a flexible and resilient identity balance.

Rebalancing one's identity should become a customary practice. Just as a business regularly audits its accounts to ensure financial health, so should individuals audit their identity balance to provide psychological and emotional well-being. Life's circumstances will inevitably change, and the need for identity rebalance will arise.

When we enter the sacred marriage union, the individual 'I' embarks on a transformational journey towards the collective 'we.' However, this beautiful amalgamation of lives brings an inherent challenge: how does one remain true to themselves while fully embracing the roles of spouse and parent? It's a nuanced dance between individuality and unity, demanding flexibility and steadfastness.

In marriage, roles and responsibilities are often pre-defined by societal norms and personal expectations. One may find themselves as the provider, the nurturer, the decision-maker, or the peacekeeper. These roles, while fulfilling, can be double-edged swords. They afford us a sense of purpose and belonging but can also confine us, slowly chipping away at our identity. The key lies in recognizing these roles as facets of our lives, not the entirety of our being. Herein lies a role of the Identity ATM: to entrust the processes that protect one's identity so they are eventually sharing and providing more richness to the relationship, not draining it.

There is a certain fluidity required to navigate this intricate landscape. We must be willing to step in and out of roles as the situation demands, all the while holding onto the core of who we are. This is not to say one should resist the natural evolution of self that marriage often incites; instead, it is about maintaining a balance between adapting to the partnership and preserving personal integrity. The artistry of this balance is in allowing oneself to grow through the roles without being consumed by them.

As the layers of spousal roles accumulate, they can sometimes overshadow the primary colors of our identity. It's essential, therefore, to take inventory of these roles periodically. Which ones serve our higher purpose and enrich our sense of self? Which ones do we perform out of obligation, and at what cost to our individuality? These questions are not asked to discard our responsibilities but to align them more closely with our true selves. In doing so, we may discover new strengths and redefine our roles in ways that resonate with our identity.

When setting boundaries, the process is both delicate and critical. Boundaries are the invisible lines that protect the sanctity of our inner selves. They enable us to say 'yes' to the relationship and 'no' to losing ourselves. Establishing boundaries in a marriage is an ongoing conversation, one that requires honesty, courage, and mutual respect. It's about expressing needs and limits, not as ultimatums but as fundamental aspects of a healthy relationship. When respected, these boundaries allow for individual growth alongside marital harmony.

Conflict in marriage is often perceived as an opposing force, a sign of dysfunction. However, when viewed through the lens of identity, conflict can be a potent indicator of where our boundaries are being challenged or our roles are becoming too restrictive. It signals that our inner selves are seeking expression and room to breathe. Resolving these conflicts shouldn't aim to return to the status quo but for a higher understanding and integration of our individualities within the marriage.

Similarly in parenting, withdrawal from one's identity becomes even more pronounced. The role of a parent is all-consuming, characterized by selfless acts of love, sacrifice, and an often-overwhelming sense of responsibility. Parenting, in its very essence, requires the giving of ourselves to our children. This exchange is not a mere transaction; it's an investment in the future, nurturing another life with the nutrients of our wisdom, values, and love.

Navigating the marriage and parenting journey while maintaining one's identity is like charting a course through an ever-changing landscape. The milestones of personal relationships can reshape the topography of selfhood, each leaving its mark as indeed as rivers carve canyons. As the years pass, the initial path one might have carved for oneself can become overgrown, the destination no longer visible through the foliage of daily commitments and sacrifices.

When we are young and want to build credit, we take out small loans to show banks they can trust us. If our payments are made on time and eventually pay it off, our credit score goes up and we are entrusted with a higher amount or a lower interest rate for future loans. In relationships, the principles are the same. We start small with trust, some even distrusting completely until trust is earned, but it is a factor, nonetheless. Once we have built up our 'trust credit', this allows us to take some chances and risks. This is reflected in asking someone to marry you, deciding to have kids, being promoted in your work.

In this complex interplay, adaptation and growth are natural and inevitable. They require a conscientious approach, an attentiveness to the ever-shifting ground beneath one's feet. Personal evolution is often subtle within a shared life, manifesting in quiet shifts in thought and emotion rather than seismic breaks from the past. The person who entered a marriage differs after years of partnership and raising children. The personal identity that once seemed so solid is now fluid, adapting to the contours of a shared existence.

This adaptation is a process of becoming, often happening incrementally, like a book's slow turn of pages. Every experience, every challenge faced together, and every joy shared writes a new line in the narrative of self. The task is to remain both author and protagonist within this story, ensuring that the narrative thread remains unbroken even as the plot twists unexpectedly.

In this sense, growth is not just a journey outward into the world but also inward, delving into the depths of one's character and capabilities. It is discovering resilience in the face of parenting trials, finding wellsprings of patience and empathy within a marriage, and learning that the individual's strength can bolster the union's power.

Part of this process is accepting the evolution of one's identity. The beliefs, values, and priorities that were once held as absolute may shift in the light of a partner's perspectives or in the act of nurturing a child. These shifts are not betrayals of self but acknowledgments of the complex nature of human identity, which is not fixed but responsive to the context in which it exists. This responsiveness should not be confused with weakness; it is the courage to relinquish rigid self-conceptions in favor of a more nuanced understanding of who one can become.

Moreover, the evolution of identity in the context of marriage and parenting requires a generous spirit of forgiveness—forgiveness for the dreams deferred, moments of self-doubt, and times when the balance between self and roles feels lost. Forgiveness allows for growth, for the recognition that each stage of life brings with it its challenges and opportunities for development.

In this evolving self-concept, one must remember the practice of revisiting and rebalancing one's identity. Life's transitions from the addition of new family members to the developmental milestones of children, from career changes to the natural aging process demand that we constantly reassess who we are and wish to be. This is not a task to be taken lightly; it requires time and space for reflection, for quiet contemplation away from the noise of daily life.

The act of revisiting one's identity can be akin to standing before a mirror, not in search of the youth one once possessed but in pursuit of the truth of one's current existence. It involves asking hard questions: Who am I now? What do I value? What brings me fulfillment and joy? These questions, while daunting, are the compass by which one can navigate the complexities of an evolving personal identity.

Rebalancing is equally vital. Just as one might adjust their stance to maintain equilibrium on a swaying surface, so must one adjust the various elements of one's life to maintain a sense of self. This can mean reallocating time, redefining success, or resetting expectations to reflect the person one has become. It might also involve renegotiating the terms of one's roles within the family, ensuring that they align with personal values and current capabilities.

Such reassessment is not an indication of failure but an act of self-preservation and self-respect. It acknowledges that the self is not sacrificed on the altar of family life but is integrated into it. The balance between personal identity and the roles of spouse and parent must be dynamic and responsive to the moment's needs without losing sight of the overarching narrative of one's life.

Considering this journey about the Identity ATM, we can further illuminate the complex transactions between personal growth, familial roles, and individual identity.

The Identity ATM is not a machine but a repository for an individual's sense of self. Every experience in marriage and parenting is akin to a transaction, some withdrawals and some deposits, impacting the balance of who we are and how we perceive ourselves. As we navigate through the stages of life, we are constantly engaged in these transactions, each altering the balance of our identity.

In the acts of adaptation and growth within a family context, we often must withdraw from our Identity ATM. We might draw from our reserves of independence when we compromise for the benefit of a partner's career move. We may withdraw from our time when our children's needs must come first. These withdrawals are essential; they represent the sacrifices that are a part of any committed relationship and the parental responsibilities of raising children.

However, these withdrawals need to be balanced by deposits to maintain a healthy sense of self. Personal growth, the inward journey of self-discovery and change, is one such deposit. Each time we learn something new about ourselves, such as the depth of our patience, the strength of our resolve, or the breadth of our empathy, we deposit into our Identity ATM.

The act of revisiting and rebalancing one's identity is crucial to the Identity ATM. It's the equivalent of a periodic account review, ensuring that the ledger of self is accurate and reflective of our current values and circumstances. It's a time to assess which transactions have benefited our sense of self and which have left us overdrawn. This is where forgiveness and self-care come into play, acting as necessary investments that protect and grow our identity capital.

As mentioned in previous chapters, self-care is a crucial deposit that provides dividends in the form of resilience and contentment. Our identity balance can be depleted without these regular deposits, leaving us feeling lost or burned out. The support of a partner, family, and friends acts as an investment from others into our account, bolstering our balance and enriching our sense of self. The feeling of 'growing apart' reflects a couple that failed to maintain a positive balance amongst the thousands of transactions in their marriage, resulting in more withdrawals than deposits.

Moreover, the relationship of marriage and parenting to the Identity ATM highlights that this is not a zero-sum game. The growth and evolution of our identity can result in a net gain for both our sense of self and our familial relationships. When we deposit new aspects of personal growth into our Identity ATM, we're not just enriching ourselves; we're enhancing the collective wealth of our family unit. Each family member's individual growth contributes to a more dynamic family identity.

In this sense, the Identity ATM's joint account is a shared resource for the relationship. The health of this account is crucial not only to our personal well-being but also to the overall health of the marital partnership and the family structure. Just as a financial joint account requires transparency, communication, and joint decision-making, the Identity ATM demands honesty, openness, and collaborative management of identity resources.

By managing the transactions of our Identity ATM with care, being mindful of the need for both withdrawals and deposits, only then can we navigate the shifting landscape of marriage and parenting without losing sight of our horizons. We keep our account balanced, ensuring that while we give generously of ourselves to our partners and children, we also invest wisely in the growth and sustenance of our identity. Through this balance, we sustain our sense of self and bring our best selves to the shared journey of family life.

Questions for Reflection:

1. What does a joint account mean, in your own words?
2. What withdrawals have been made from a joint account that has influenced major life decisions?
3. What are some methods to discern situations depositing/withdrawing from your personal and joint accounts?
4. Who are some of the stakeholders in the various joint accounts that you are in?
5. What proactive steps can I take to enhance the relationships using the Identity ATM?
6. Who are you intentional about making healthy deposits into their Identity ATM?
7. How do I balance giving others emotional support and preserving my emotional well-being? How have my relationships been affected due to guilt or shame?

The Brain Behind Your Identity

Chapter Concept: The inner workings of our brains and corresponding neurons directly link to our ability to receive the proper information to construct our personal narrative and identity.

Chapter Strategy for Enrichment: Identify how the brain relates to identity formation, correlating how various parts of the brain work with how we express ourselves in words and actions.

As we journey through the intricacies of our emotional world, one element stands out in its significance: the balance of our mental and emotional well-being is linked to how our brains operate. Much like a financial balance sheet reflects the ability to refine an organization, our identity balance sheet offers insights into our inner state. Proficiency in eliminating balance deficits and instituting practices for enrichment and rejuvenation underscore why we should develop self-awareness. Our Identity ATM will shift with cultural and community trends. Anticipating and adapting to these changes is a focal point of using the Identity ATM.

The internal transactions are ultimately a transformation of the identity's expression. For example, an athlete who fails to win the championship may express themselves through guilt, saying, "I failed." Guilt, in a deciphering manner, highlights the truth of the situation, thus supplying a starting point for behavior management. The behavior shift may be to practice more, get more sleep the night before the game, or ask for learning support from a mentor or coach. If the Identity ATM lacks funds of self-esteem and confidence, the athlete who fails to win is susceptible to shame, which includes expressions such as, "I am a failure" or, "I'll never get this right." By actively allocating funds of self-esteem and confidence to the Identity ATM, it will, in return, bestow value upon one's expression. The positive expression of "I failed" is led to further proffering, becoming "I failed, but I can do better."

For centuries, the human brain has been front and center of curiosity and scientific study. It controls our movements, governs our thoughts, and, most intriguingly, is our identity's birthplace. The interplay between the brain and how we express ourselves contributes to how we perceive the world, interact with others, and envision ourselves. As we begin to unpack this idea, it becomes evident that one must first delve into how the brain develops ideas. We must do so before fully appreciating the depth of human emotions and cognitive behavior.

At its core, the brain is an organ of billions of neurons that communicate via very intricate networks. Each region and part of the brain has a specific function, processing everything from basic survival instincts to philosophical thoughts; amid this supercomputer or paperweight sitting on our shoulders (depending on how well it is used), thoughts are created, emotions emerge as a result of those thoughts, and an added depth and color to the human experience is formed.

The limbic system, aka the emotional brain, nestled deep within the brain, comprises various components, including the amygdala, hippocampus, and hypothalamus. The amygdala determines the perception of emotions. Fear and anger are often associated with the amygdala, with anger being a secondary emotion to fear. It helps individuals work through threats and prepares the body to respond by confronting the danger, fleeing from it, or not doing anything. This is commonly known as 'fight, flight, or freeze'.

The hippocampus is the component of memory formation. Emotions and memories are deeply meshed, similar to taste and smell. Please think of how a particular song can transport someone back to a specific moment in their life, recalling the same powerful emotions. This is the hippocampus at work, associating feelings with memories and ensuring they are stored together. Then, there's the hypothalamus, which functions in our mood and arousal. It's responsible for releasing various hormones that can affect mood. The hypothalamus moderates a surge of adrenaline during a moment of fear or the release of oxytocin during bonding moments.

The relationship between the brain and identity, and correspondingly, one's emotions, is not confined to the limbic system. The prefrontal cortex, residing in the brain's frontal lobe, involves decision-making, reasoning, and regulating emotions. It helps individuals think before they act, assess situations rationally, and even practice empathy. The prefrontal cortex development, especially during early childhood ages and adolescence, factors into and essentially mirrors emotional maturity.

The brain operates like a department head meeting. The prefrontal cortex is at the head of the table as Chief Decision-Making Officer, receiving information via neuron messages from other parts of the brain sitting around the table, such as the amygdala and the hippocampus, each representing their departments well. The prefrontal cortex then takes all the information and decides what to do with it. Now, if you're under the age of 25 years old, your Chief Decision-Maker, generally, is not quite as experienced or capable of clearly hearing the information coming from around the table, so your choices may not always be the healthiest ones. This essentially disrupts portions of what is sought when processing your thoughts and the emotions derived from your thoughts.

Emotions are not just abstract feelings; they have a biochemical basis. Neurotransmitters, chemical messengers in the brain, are pivotal in regulating mood and emotions. Dopamine, for instance, is often associated with pleasure and reward. A surge of dopamine injects feelings of happiness and satisfaction. On the other hand, serotonin is part of our mood stabilization, and imbalances in serotonin levels are linked to mood disorders like depression.

Furthermore, emotions are not static but highly responsive to external stimuli and internal thoughts. External factors, such as social interactions, environmental changes, or even a piece of music, can trigger emotional responses. Internal characteristics, like thoughts, beliefs, or memories, can influence emotions.

In the context of social interactions, mirror neurons deserve mention. These specialized neurons fire in response to someone else performing the same function. Counselors sometimes do this in counseling, such as when a counselee crosses their legs, the counselor also crosses their legs. They play a role in empathy, helping individuals resonate with others' emotions. When you feel joy seeing a loved one succeed or pain seeing them in distress, mirror neurons are at play.

The brain-emotion relationship, as you can see now, has an impenetrable impact on mental health. Conditions like depression, anxiety, bipolar disorder, and many others have roots in the brain's structures and neurotransmitter imbalances. Expertise in the brain-emotion connection is dominant in treating these conditions and locating insights into therapeutic interventions and potential treatments. The interplay between the brain and emotions is also evident in the realm of learning. Emotionally charged experiences tend to be more memorable. Therefore, educators often use emotional hooks or connections to make lessons more memorable. Emotions can enhance attention, motivation, and memory during the learning process.

It's also worth noting that the brain-emotion relationship is bidirectional. While the brain influences emotions, emotions can also impact the brain. Massive amounts of research document the fact that chronic stress or prolonged negative emotions literally change the shape, size, and processing functions of the brain. For instance, chronic stress impacts decision-making and emotional regulation.

The relationship between the brain, its functions, and your identity is a symphony that adds depth to the human experience, influencing perceptions, actions, and interactions. This relationship is not just an academic pursuit, but one that exposes what it means to be human. As neuroscience unravels the mysteries of the brain, it is highlighting the interconnectedness of thought, feeling, and experience. Embracing this interconnectedness allows a richer consideration of oneself, others, and the world. The relationship between the brain and our emotional assets and liabilities highlights the captivating human experience we call 'being torn'. Delving into neuroscience, it becomes evident how our emotional wealth and debts are reflected within the brain's functions and structures.

Emotional assets, including resilience, empathy, and optimism, are deeply rooted in these neural pathways and networks. For instance, an individual with a well-developed prefrontal cortex often displays better emotional regulation, an asset in handling life's ups and downs. This emotional regulation acts as a buffer, ensuring that the individual can maintain equilibrium despite external adversities, making decisions that are not purely reactionary but rather well-thought-out.

Furthermore, the connections between the prefrontal cortex and the amygdala bring a balanced emotional response. When faced with a threat, a robust relationship ensures that while the amygdala might trigger an emotional reaction, the prefrontal cortex can assess the situation and modulate the response appropriately.

On the other hand, emotional liabilities, such as impulsivity, anxiety, or chronic pessimism, can be traced back to imbalances or disruptions in the brain's functioning. For instance, an overactive amygdala can result in heightened fear responses or anxiety. Without the mediating influence of the prefrontal cortex, such individuals might find themselves frequently trapped in a cycle of stress and worry. Furthermore, repeated exposure to stressors can reinforce these neural pathways, making breaking out of these emotional patterns increasingly challenging. Chronic stress has been shown to reduce the size of the prefrontal cortex, further exacerbating emotional liabilities and making it harder for individuals to practice emotional regulation.

Neuroplasticity raises hope in this scenario. It implies that emotional assets can be improved and liabilities mitigated with consistent effort and the right interventions. Meditation, cognitive-behavioral therapy, and even certain forms of physical exercise have promoted neuroplasticity, enabling individuals to strengthen their emotional assets and reduce liabilities. To regulate emotions better, practice mindfulness that can enhance the connectivity between the amygdala and the prefrontal cortex. This is but one method to engage syncing your brain with your Identity ATM. The transactions that take place outside of your mind are eventually submitted for processing and record keeping inside your mind.

Responses to Deficits

Before embarking on the rectification journey, gaining a deep understanding of our emotional deficits is paramount. When we talk about emotional imbalances, sure signs are quite illuminating. For instance, persistent fatigue that doesn't directly result from physical exertion might hint at an underlying emotional drain. It's more than just feeling tired; it's an exhaustion that seeps into one's spirit and mind, making even mundane tasks insurmountable.

Another revealing sign is the act of avoidance. This isn't merely about dodging certain situations or people. It's a deeper, more encompassing behavior where individuals might steer clear of introspection, evading their feelings and thoughts. This avoidance, often rooted in fear or anxiety, paints a clear picture of emotional imbalance. It's as if confronting certain situations or emotions might unleash a torrent of feelings one believes one cannot handle.

Furthermore, it's a red flag when emotional outbursts occur frequently and seemingly without reason. Picture a scenario where reactions are inexplicably intense, not aligning with the gravity of the situation. Such disproportionate emotional responses often act as windows to deeper, underlying issues that haven't been addressed. Then, there's the dwindling flame of motivation. We've all had moments of lethargy, but it's alarming when there's a consistent and noticeable dip in enthusiasm or passion. This is about something other than the routine ebb and flow of energy but a sustained lack of drive, even for things that once ignited passion and excitement. When such a decline happens without any discernible external cause, it's often signaling emotional weariness.

Lastly, feelings of emptiness can creep in despite the bustling world filled with accomplishments and celebrations. A profound sense of unfulfillment lingers, casting shadows over achievements and milestones. No matter how glittering the external accolades, there's a persistent void, a sense that something core to self is missing. Contrary to the apparent successes, this chronic void is a poignant sign of an emotional deficit.

Rectifying emotional imbalances will be more challenging than necessary when avoiding the signs and not taking the first and predominant step to healing. Only with awareness can one immerse in the landscape of emotions and strive for balance and well-being.

Take the journey towards emotional well-being. It requires a combination of self-care practices and professional support. One of the most significant steps one can take is to seek therapy or counseling. Professional guidance offers a wealth of insights into understanding and addressing issues that are often deeply embedded in our psyche. Therapists can help in profiling complex emotional patterns and provide strategies for tackling them effectively.

In tandem with professional help, incorporating mindfulness and meditation into our daily routine can be incredibly beneficial. These practices are not mere trends but are established methods for enhancing emotional awareness. Mindfulness helps individuals to remain present and attentive to their current experiences, allowing for the early detection and management of emotional imbalances before they escalate. With its roots in various traditions, meditation offers a time-tested pathway to tranquility and a balanced mind.

Physical fitness is another cornerstone of emotional health. Regular exercise is not just about keeping the body fit; it also plays a critical role in maintaining brain health. A balanced diet and adequate rest are equally important, as they fuel both the body and the brain. The link between the physical body and emotional health does come with variables, such as our body type, medical concerns, and medical history, but when we take care of our bodies, we set a solid foundation for our emotional well-being, similarly discussed in this book regarding the habits of sleeping well and drinking enough water. With anything, the best approach is to find the right bank that supports the value and deposits necessary for the healthiest you.

The environments we immerse ourselves in and the company we keep can profoundly impact our emotional health. Much has been discussed in terms of connections. In correlation to emotional assets specifically, they are often necessary to limit exposure to toxic elements, whether they are people who drain our energy, situations that consistently cause distress, or media that feed negativity. Protecting our mental space from such toxicity is a form of self-care that preserves our emotional reserves for more constructive and fulfilling engagements. Establishing a milieu where one feels supported and connected can significantly impact one's sense of self and emotional security. Communities, whether formed around hobbies, beliefs, or shared experiences, offer a sense of belonging. They provide a network of support and comfort during challenging times and are the easiest way to learn a new skill. Being surrounded by individuals who understand and share similar journeys can make the path to well-being less daunting and more rewarding.

In essence, the path to emotional well-being is not linear or the same for everyone. It is a personalized journey that combines the wisdom of professional guidance with the healing power of self-care practices. Each step, whether it's seeking therapy, practicing mindfulness, or building community connections, plays a vital role in nurturing the emotional self. We can hope to achieve a balanced and fulfilling emotional life through this holistic approach.

To enhance the effectiveness of one's Identity ATM, there must be a primary focus on the emotional assets that come from discipline, motivation, and inspiration. Discipline, motivation, and inspiration are the trinity of forces that drive us toward the achievement of our goals. They are the wind, the rudder, and the sails of our personal success vessels, steering us through the tumultuous seas of daily life. Understanding how these elements work together to propel us to the finish line of our aspirations requires a deep dive into the nature of each and the symbiotic relationship they share.

Discipline: The Foundation of Achievement

Discipline is often seen as the bedrock of goal attainment. It is the structured approach to our daily actions, the unwavering commitment to regularity and order, and the power to stay the course even when the initial excitement has waned. Discipline is about setting up systems and habits that eliminate the need for constant decision-making and willpower.

Imagine discipline as the inner framework that holds up the building of achievement. Without it, the structure will eventually crumble, no matter how grand the design or how profound the motivation is. Discipline ensures that we get out of bed every morning and work on our tasks, regardless of how we feel. It is the force that keeps us moving step by step, day by day, towards our long-term goals. It's what makes us stick to our schedules, meet our deadlines, and consistently chip away at the tasks that lead to success.

The power of discipline lies in its ability to transform actions into habits. When an action becomes habitual, it requires less mental effort to initiate, making it more likely to be completed even on days when motivation is low. Discipline breeds consistency, and consistency is key to progress. Our identity takes on the mannerisms of being disciplined as well. This is extremely beneficial when examining our thoughts before they become feelings. Most feelings are second nature, but when we have completely funded a disciplined ability to process transactions, we prevent all forms of unhealthy emotional and mental transactions. Think of a bank teller who has been on the job for years and can easily process deposits. That has been developed by the discipline and confidence associated with the repetition of doing the right things. Our Identity ATM could develop discipline just like that. It requires practice, repetition, and intentionality.

Motivation: Marathon Living

While discipline is associated with conditioning habits, motivation is the energy that powers our actions. The internal drive propels us to take the first step and the subsequent ones after that. Motivation is often emotional, tied to our desires, our dreams, and the rewards that await us. Consider the motivation required to run a marathon. Of course, the discipline to stick to a training routine will allow you to accomplish the feat, but motivation is what connects you to your behaviors. The vision of crossing the finish line keeps us lacing up our shoes and heading out to train day after day.

Motivation can come from various sources: a personal challenge we've set for ourselves, the desire to improve our lives, or the aspiration to achieve something that we deem important. It can be intrinsic, driven by internal rewards like personal growth and self-satisfaction, or extrinsic, propelled by external rewards, such as recognition or financial gain. Motivation intersects with the Identity ATM in one wanting to express their identity in a positive and healthy manner while maintaining as much control as possible over who they are known to be. However, motivation can be fleeting. It's often present in abundance at the start of a new venture but can wane as time goes on and obstacles arise. That's where discipline steps in to carry us through the lows. But motivation is not to be discounted; it is the spark that ignites the fire of action. When harnessed effectively, it can be a powerful force that fuels our journey toward goal completion. The motivation marathon perfectly relates to how runners hit the mental wall in their quest for 26.2 miles. If one only verbalizes their desires but doesn't connect them with disciplines toward a goal, there will be no finish line crossing.

Inspiration: The Breath of Possibility

Inspiration is the breath that gives life to our dreams. It is often the catalyst for new ideas, the lightbulb moment that pushes us to embark on a journey towards a goal. Inspiration is found from within. It is characterized by a moment of clarity, a sudden surge of possibility, making us believe in our ability to achieve something greater. The Identity ATM is a proponent for inspiration to form. The expression of our identity is intricately linked to creativity and is often the source of innovative solutions to problems. It drives us to think outside the box, see beyond the ordinary, and imagine what could be. It's the force that compels us to set goals in the first place, providing a vision of an ideal future or a state of being that we wish to reach.

Unlike discipline and motivation, inspiration cannot be easily summoned. It tends to strike spontaneously, in moments of quiet reflection or in the presence of something truly awe-inspiring. However, one can create an environment conducive to inspiration by seeking new experiences, engaging with diverse ideas, and opening oneself up to the world's wonders.

The Interplay Between Discipline, Motivation, and Inspiration

The journey to the finish line of our goals is rarely a straight path. It's a winding road filled with peaks and valleys, and the combination of discipline, motivation, and inspiration keeps us moving forward. They each play a role at different times and under different circumstances. The deposits we receive from our bank of choice are influential in where and how we navigate toward the goal of a healthy expression of our identity.

When we begin a new endeavor, inspiration often jumps to the forefront. The voice whispers, "You can do this; you can be more." It gives us the initial concept or goal to strive toward. Motivation then takes this idea and turns it into action. It fills us with the desire to make the first move, to take the leap into the unknown.

As we progress, the initial high of inspiration and the eager push of motivation may begin to fade. This is where discipline takes over. Discipline is the steady hand that guides us through the monotony of the middle, the part of the journey where progress can seem slow and the end is not yet in sight. It is the commitment to keep moving forward, even when the initial excitement has passed.

There will be times when motivation surges back, often sparked by small successes along the way or the encouragement of others. These boosts are invaluable, providing bursts of speed that propel us closer to our end goal. However, it's discipline that ensures these boosts are not wasted and that the energy of motivation is channeled into productive action.

And throughout it all, inspiration continues to play a role, albeit subtler. It is in the background, reminding us of the bigger picture and why we set out on this path in the first place. It renews our spirit when challenges arise and provides fresh perspectives that can help us overcome obstacles.

Crossing the Finish Line

As we approach the finish line, the harmony of discipline, motivation, and inspiration gets us there. Discipline ensures we don't stray from the path. Motivation compels us to keep pushing, especially in the final stretch. Inspiration allows us to cross the line with our heads held high, ready to dream of the next challenge.

Achieving our goals is not just about the moment of success; it's about the journey it takes to get there. It's about the lessons learned through discipline, the energy harnessed through motivation, and the possibilities uncovered through inspiration. When we understand and embrace the roles of these three elements, we unlock the potential not just to reach the finish line but to cross it in a way that sets the stage for even greater achievements in the future.

The journey of achieving our goals is, therefore, not just about the attainment of a desired outcome. It is a testament to our ability to harness the inner workings of our psyche when we have the discipline to remain steadfast, the motivation to pursue our passions, and the inspiration to dream beyond our current realities. These forces get us across the finish line and redefine the limits of what that line can be. This is where emotional rebalancing has an impact on our Identity ATM. Adding a small, daily discipline to improve our well-being can surge our health's value.

Case Studies: Transformation through Emotional Rebalancing

To showcase the impact of rectifying emotional deficits, let's explore a couple of real-life journeys:

1.	Liam, a high-performing professional, constantly felt drained. Despite accolades and achievements, a sense of fulfillment eluded him. His emotional balance sheet revealed high liabilities from past familial traumas and current work stressors. By seeking therapy and engaging in community volunteer work, Liam built emotional assets, purpose, and emotional rejuvenation through quality connections and having a purpose to pursue.

2.	A homemaker and mother, Priya often felt overwhelmed and unappreciated. Chronic fatigue and emotional outbursts became frequent characteristics of her emotional deficits; she began journaling, took up meditation, and joined a hobby class. These activities introduced her to an outlet as a supportive community. Priya's journey from emotional exhaustion to rejuvenation showcases the power of intentional rebalancing.

Reflecting on these two emotional balance sheets, what rectification is essential? What is equally vital to future-proof their emotional advancements? Some long-term strategies include continuous learning, regular check-ins, and participating in joyful activities. What other types of engagements come to mind?

Questions for reflection:

1. How do prolonged periods of stress or trauma affect the brain's structure and, subsequently, our emotional health?
2. Can regular mindfulness practices, such as meditation, alter the brain's structure or function to enhance emotional resilience? If yes, how so?
3. How does the amygdala, the brain's center for processing emotions, influence our reactions to emotional stimuli, and how can we train it for better emotional responses?
4. How do our brain's cognitive biases, such as confirmation bias, impact our emotional perceptions and reactions to events around us?
5. How can understanding the brain's default mode network help reduce rumination and promote emotional well-being?
6. How do the connections between the prefrontal cortex and other brain regions affect emotional regulation and decision-making?

Personal Identity and Organizational Resilience

Chapter Concept: The Identity ATM is not limited to individuals, but organizations made up of people. Healthy employees create healthy organizations.

Chapter Strategy for Enrichment: Teach leaders at any level how to live in the disparity between their respective organizational culture and climate, creating resilient organizations and thriving in a fast-paced, changing world.

In the progressive and modern corporate world, two forms of resilience have become paramount: personal resilience, or the individual's ability to bounce back from adversity and, as discussed throughout this book, including the ability to learn from that adversity, and organizational resilience, the capacity to anticipate and adapt to incremental change and sudden disruptions.

These two forms of resilience intersect, with personal resilience playing a foundational role in building robust organizations. But how do these two relate, and how do the disparities in organizational culture expectations affect shared perceptions? Stagnate in the discussion on organizational resilience is determining the role of emotions for employees. This chapter seeks to explore the inactivity of organizational leaders to highlight the role of emotional resilience.

The Personal and Organizational Resilience Connection

Individual resilience is characterized by adaptability, flexibility, and a balanced posture between positive and realistic outlooks. Similarly, resilient organizations can weather the storms of their industry, adapt to new situations, and come out stronger. The link between the two is straightforward: organizations are made up of individuals. When employees demonstrate resilience, the organization naturally benefits. Every time an individual overcomes a hurdle learns a new skill, or can mobilize in a personal crisis, they yield an addition to their collective reservoir of strength and adaptability. However, there are always pitfalls to getting stronger.

Consider today's digital era, as almost everyone can relate to the experience of receiving a notification about a software update for their smartphone. While these updates may sometimes feel like minor inconveniences, they optimize the phone's performance, fix bugs, and introduce new features. This concept of regular 'updates' is more comprehensive than technology alone. Analogously, individuals and organizations need periodic 'updates' to function efficiently, adapt to changing environments, and reach their fullest potential.

Like a smartphone, people and organizations function with multiple components working in tandem. Over time, with wear and tear, changing external conditions, and the introduction of new tools and technologies, there's a need to recalibrate, refine, and revamp certain elements to ensure optimal performance. Not only is the old equipment left behind, but also the remnants of an employee's connection to 'how things used to be.' If the employee is not part of the change management process, their identity will likely stay there. The biggest issue with organizational changes and the inability to get buy-in comes when leadership does not decipher how the employee's confidence and self-esteem are impacted.

Organizations and people are consistently faced with the reality of new environments and forced to adjust how transactions are handled. There is tension between the 'old school' method of living and the cultural shifts happening all around. Leaders and employees must learn how to 'read the room' and trust that they can take employees in a new direction, not based on comfort but on competency.

Developing Contextual Intelligence Nourishes Organizations

Building employee resilience isn't just about dispensing gym memberships and encouraging work-life balance, though those are essential components. Indeed, emotional intelligence affords positive developments, but there is a growing emphasis on contextual intelligence. Creating an environment where employees feel valued, understood, and empowered is key to harvesting significance. Training and development, mentoring, and a culture of continuous learning invested in the staff are paid back with interest. The unspoken agreement lies in the development that impacts one's personal life as much as one's professional one.

When employees are developed, this not only highlights technical skills they bring to the table but also interpersonal skills, such as problem-solving abilities and conflict resolution, but also innovative thinking, prioritization skills, and resourcing. As employees grow, they bring fresh perspectives and energy, invigorating the organization and ensuring it remains agile to do things more efficiently incrementally. A well-rounded, developed employee is an asset to their personal growth and the overarching success of the organization. This also allows employees to absorb changes and consider their work as something they are administering the difference themselves.

The Disparity Within Organizational Culture - Expectations vs. Reality

While the idea of nurturing a positive organizational culture is universally captivating, there is often a stark disparity between what's propagated from the leaders' expectations and the shared experience by employees. Leaders might espouse values of transparency, inclusivity, and collaboration, but if employees feel there's a lack of genuine communication, feel excluded from decision-making, or work in silos. A gap exists between expectation and reality. An employee's ability to maintain coping mechanisms translates to an organization's ability to maintain psychological safety and emotional security in that culture.

This disparity can be attributed to various factors. Sometimes, leadership may be genuinely unaware of the shared experiences of their employees. In other instances, superficial efforts fail to manifest their desired positive culture due to insincerity and depth. Additionally, in larger organizations, the abuse of authority at lower levels and discrepancies between departments or teams undermine the organization's culture with its subculture.

Bridging the Gap with Shared Perceptions and Experiences

Leaders must live in the disparity gap between their organizational culture's top-down, expected values and principles and the bottom-up, shared experiences and perceptions of the organizational climate. Addressing the disparity requires open dialogue. Organizations can start bridging the gap by encouraging employees to utilize their perspectives and experiences in shaping the future. This means conducting annual surveys, holding focus group discussions, and genuinely listening, resulting in a culture where feedback is encouraged and acted upon. Additionally, shared experiences, such as team-building activities, cross-departmental projects, or organization-wide initiatives, can help unify the culture. When individuals from various teams or departments collaborate, they bring their unique experiences into the mix, helping to build a more cohesive organizational identity.

Human Capital and Identity

Human capital refers to the economic value that an individual's abilities, knowledge, and experience contribute to an organization or economy. It is a concept that encapsulates the intangible collective resources possessed by individuals, such as education, health, expertise, and skills, which can be invested in and enhanced through further education and training. These are very effective methods to mitigate or eliminate the disparity in an organization's culture. Even more so, recruitment and retention increase and coincide with human factors and human capital investment increases.

The intersection of human capital and personal identity is particularly significant in the modern workplace. As individuals, we bring our personal identities into the professional realm. Our background, culture, and life experiences inform how we approach our work, solve problems, and interact with colleagues. In turn, our professional experiences contribute to our personal identity, shaping our self-perception and our perception by others.

Human capital theory suggests that investment in people with education, training, and health care, etc. enhances an individual's productivity and earnings over a lifetime. This theory implies a strong link between human capital development and economic growth in addition to the company's profitability with further developed employees. Governments and organizations, therefore, focus on policies and practices that can build and utilize human capital to drive economic expansion and innovation.

Personal identity plays a critical role in the development of human capital. The choices that individuals make regarding their education and career paths are deeply intertwined with their sense of self. For instance, someone who identifies strongly with a particular social cause may pursue a career in non-profit organizations or social work. This alignment between personal identity and professional endeavor can lead to greater job satisfaction and productivity, as the individual will likely be more engaged and committed to their work.

However, the relationship between personal identity and human capital is challenging. The digital age has brought new dimensions and dynamics. The rise of social media and online platforms allows individuals to craft and curate their personal and professional identities in unprecedented ways. Digital footprints can enhance an individual's human capital by showcasing their skills and expertise to a broader audience. Conversely, they can also pose risks to personal identity, as the line between personal and professional life blurs.

Human capital policies and an employee's personal identity are very influential to the organization's resilience. Put more bluntly, taking care of employees builds organizational resilience. Aside from the basics of conducting meetings well, offering annual reviews, and offering competitive pay, organizational resilience is, below the surface, connected to one's identity. Recognizing this interplay is essential for organizations, economies, and societies at large aiming to foster growth, innovation, and inclusion. The challenge lies in ensuring personal identity is respected and leveraged to enhance the cultivation of human capital, not impede it.

The overlap of human capital and personal identity is ultimately the inner workings of behavioral economics and organizational psychology. People in professional careers are drawn to see their work as an extension of themselves. They are drawn to unique aspects of their organizational culture. This is similar to why schools have mascots. This gives students and alumni an identity with particular characteristics to draw upon. An organization's culture is a mascot that should be used to rally the employees to express themselves with related behaviors.

The connection between personal and organizational resilience is undeniable. As individuals become more resilient, so does the overall readiness that ensures organizations can weather storms and emerge stronger. Investing in employee development benefits not only the individuals but also the organization. However, addressing the disparities in an individual's expectations and reality may default to aligning values with ground realities. Your employees have accounts with you, the Bank of Employment, and each transaction through training and professional development, mentoring, and providing feedback make deposits into their Identity ATM.

The path to building resilience, both personal and organizational, is complex. It requires introspection, feedback, adaptability, and a genuine commitment to growth. But the rewards that derive from a thriving, vibrant, and resilient organization are worth the effort. In the essence of the business landscape, organizations often prioritize factors like strategy, technology, and innovation, overlooking a fundamental component that underpins all these areas related to the well-being of their employees. But in an era where the lines between personal and professional life are becoming increasingly blurred, and the global workforce faces unprecedented crossroads, emotional well-being is no longer a luxury; it is necessary.

If you're reading this chapter and struggling to make the connection between a person's quest to infer all the facets of their identity or perhaps wonder why an employer should be concerned with their employees' emotional well-being, make the connection to the why. When employees are emotionally stable and content, their efficiency scales to new heights. They are more focused, make fewer errors, and exhibit heightened creativity. This is not mere conjecture. Emotional well-being correlates with improved cognitive function, decision-making, and problem-solving abilities.

Emotionally healthy employees also tend to be more fastened to their respective roles. Engagement goes beyond mere job satisfaction; it either increases the level of contentment, where one finds peace in the job, or promulgates one's passion and genuine interest to where one finds ways to give back to the industry. A focused and compelled employee doesn't just do the minimum required but goes the extra mile, innovating, improving processes, and supporting the forward-leaning momentum of the organization. Further discussion on this topic of identifying and removing barriers to growth and integrating healthy boundaries will be discussed in the next chapter, further exploring the connection of healthy employees creating healthy organizations.

Contextualizing Efforts through IQ and EQ

Employees with a high connection to their identity often possess high IQ and EQ traits. They can read the room during meetings, empathize with clients, and collaborate more effectively with teammates. They become adept at sensing the underlying movements in organizational conditions, enabling them to filter situations with discernment. This skill of contextualizing is invaluable in today's diverse and globalized workplace. When teams across different geographies, cultures, and backgrounds collaborate, the potential for misunderstandings is rife. A combination of intellect and emotional awareness bridges gaps between where the organization has been and where they are headed.

The Crucial Role of Leadership

Leaders play an instrumental role in stewarding an environment that expands the expressions of one's identity. When leaders prioritize emotional, mental, physical, and spiritual wellness, it sends a clear message to the employees: their well-being matters. Leaders who distinguish these facets of health tend to accentuate their organizational policies and practices geared towards fostering a holistic sense of well-being. They promote a setting where seeking help is not just accepted but encouraged. Such leaders presume that for their organization to thrive, its employees must flourish through the problems that arise.

Additionally, when leaders are inclusive of the transactions affecting themselves and how the Identity ATM works personally, they are better equipped to handle crises, guide their teams, and make strategic decisions for their career and organization's future. The human element is knowing their Identity ATM, and they are either making deposits or withdrawals, overshadowing everything. The leaders who have not done the work on their Identity ATM are often despised as they equate to a roller coaster of emotion. You are still discerning the mood for each day once they show up. They need to realize that behind every email, report, or project is a human being with emotions, aspirations, and, hopefully, a vision or purpose. By not considering these aspects, leaders miss the opportunity to create a bond of trust and loyalty with their employees.

Reaping the Benefits of a Holistic Approach

Organizations that champion the identity of their employees and their mental, emotional, and spiritual well-being don't just have happier employees; they witness tangible results. Reduced absenteeism, lower turnover rates, higher employee satisfaction scores, and improved overall productivity are just a few of the outcomes. These organizations become magnets for top-talent recruits. In an age where the battle to acquire and retain talent is fierce, being known as an organization that values its employees' well-being can be a prominent differentiator.

But the benefits aren't limited to internal power. Organizational stakeholders also prefer associating with a positive culture and values that transcend internal rewards and, in the long run, enhance the organization's brand equity. As the world evolves and adjustments like remote working bring upon digital fatigue, the resilience reservoir of employees will be tested repeatedly.

The mantra for success must be clear: Healthy employees create healthy organizations. Organizations that embrace this philosophy, the inextricable link between emotional well-being and efficiency, are establishing performance parameters and benchmarks for others to follow.

Questions for Reflection:

1. How do my personal resilience strategies align with those promoted within my organization, and where do I see opportunities for synergy or growth?
2. How does my organization respond in moments of adversity, and how does that mirror or differ from my approach to adversity?
3. How would I describe the current state of our organizational culture?
4. What proactive steps can I take to enhance my emotional well-being, and how can I advocate for similar organizational initiatives?
5. How does our organization prioritize its employees' emotional stamina, and how does this impact overall organizational performance and culture?
6. Reflecting on personal experiences and observations, how have emotionally nourished employees positively impacted the team, project outcomes, and the broader organizational culture?

Barriers and Boundaries Resilience Leadership

Chapter Concept: The cultural emphasis and connection of personal and organizational resilience.

Chapter Strategy for Enrichment: Understand the Identity ATM's interrelatedness with the organizational context.

Sometimes our identity is impacted more from the withdrawals from our identity compared to the deposits in our lives. Those major withdrawals I am referring to here is labeled by all sorts of names. Those include adversity, trauma, rejection, uncertainty, betrayal, isolation, among a long list of others associated with loss. Our identity is not revealed in moments we escape reality. It is easy to feel brave when strapped into a roller coaster, knowing the ride will be over in ninety seconds. It is easy to feel adventurous on a cruise ship where every detail is managed, and every risk is carefully controlled. These experiences may be enjoyable, but they often do not shape who we are. They do not test our character, nor do they force us to define what we truly value.

Real identity is formed in loss. Loss of status, loss of relationships, loss of job security. Remember those banks that deposit into our well-being from back in chapter one? When we lose those banks, when there is no safety net of savings, that is the time and place we discover what we are made of. Who we are is not found in curated experiences designed to entertain or distract us. Our true identity is found in the unexpected, the unfiltered, and the uncontrollable. The way we respond to pressure, failure, loss, and uncertainty is what reveals the foundation of which we have built our identity. Adverse moments of loss, despair, confusion, and grief not only expose who we truly are, they also shape us if we allow them.

Adversity forces a decision. We can resist the hardship as though it were an unwelcome intruder or we can embrace it as a defining force. Those who refuse to engage with difficulty often find themselves without a clear sense of self and/or safety. They drift and are shaped more by circumstances than by conviction. Those who confront adversity with purpose and reflection develop a more resilient identity. Resilient people align their actions with values even when the pressure is immense.

In this chapter, we will explore how identity is forged through adversity. We will look at how hardship strips away distractions, leaving behind only what is essential. We will examine how struggle refines our values and forces us to decide what we will stand for and what we will not compromise on. Finally, we will consider how adversity demands action. It should be noted that not compromising means requiring ourselves to live in alignment with our beliefs. True identity is not a product of comfort or ease.

Adversity strips away the unnecessary and exposes what truly matters. What once felt urgent fades into the background and leaves only the undeniable reality of our core priorities. Comfort and convenience and entertainment may offer temporary relief, but they do not define us. When life becomes difficult distractions lose their hold and force us to confront deeper questions of identity and purpose.

Hardship does more than challenge us. It clarifies who we are. It forces us to separate what is meaningful from what is fleeting. Adversity tests whether our values are deeply rooted or merely convenient. Integrity and perseverance and faith are easy to claim when unchallenged but only when they come at a cost do, we see whether they are truly part of our identity or just words we use to describe ourselves.

Struggle demands a choice. We can resist and hope for easier circumstances or we can embrace difficulty as a chance to refine who we are. Those who resist often drift and feel lost without understanding why. Those who face adversity head-on gain direction. They do not wait for clarity to find them. They allow hardship to shape it. They recognize that identity is not given but built through action and endurance.

Emotional Equity in the Workplace

Personal adversity does not stay confined to personal life. It follows employees into the workplace, affecting focus, performance, and engagement. Organizations cannot afford to ignore the reality that employees carry struggles with them. Leaders who recognize this understand that resilience is not just an individual trait but a collective one. Emotional equity in the workplace is built when leaders proactively acknowledge the weight employees carry and create an environment where they feel seen rather than dismissed. This is not about lowering expectations or making excuses. It is about fostering a culture where employees can navigate hardship without fear of being devalued. Leaders who invest in emotional equity strengthen the foundation of their teams, ensuring that resilience is not just a personal skill but an organizational advantage.

There are numerous specifics to highlight when speaking on the topic of emotional equity in the workplace. First, how I define it. Emotional equity in the workplace is the investment an employee makes into their work environment, career, and professional relationships to build and exchange respect, understanding, and value within the organization or community. This is about individuals contributing to a workplace culture that values who they are, not just what they do.

A leader does not exist to avoid hardship in the performance of duties for an organization. A leader exists to navigate through them. Barriers or obstacles arise from a variety of ways that challenges a leader's competency. Such as when an employee struggles, leadership is not about offering empty encouragement. It is about stepping in with clarity and action. Leaders set the tone for how adversity is handled. They can ignore it and let employees feel isolated or they can acknowledge it and provide the support needed to move forward. A leader does not have to fix every problem, but they must recognize when hardship threatens the strength of the team.

An organization rises or falls based on the resilience of its people. Employees facing hardship bring that weight into their work. A leader who refuses to see this allows stress and uncertainty to spread like wildfire. A leader who takes responsibility builds trust that offsets the viral impact insecurity brings into the culture. If you are a leader, please know you do not need all the answers. At a minimum, what employees are looking for in times of adversity is stability. Be the presence in difficult moments that determines whether employees see themselves as valued or expendable.

Hardship reveals the true nature of leadership and the culture. Anyone can lead when everything runs smoothly. Real leadership shows up when pressure builds. Employees do not remember the leader who spoke about resilience. They remember the leader who demonstrated it. When leaders act with integrity during difficult times, they give employees permission to do the same. When they avoid tough conversations or abandon struggling employees, they create a culture where people do the same.

Support does not mean solving every problem. It means standing firm when people need direction. A leader who listens without dismissing. A leader who challenges without breaking. A leader who remains present when others want to retreat. These are the ones who create lasting impact. Hardship will always exist. The question is not whether employees will face it. The question is whether they will have a leader who walks through it with them.

It was intentional for me to integrate the organizational context in this chapter. Why? Well, quite frankly because most of the stress and adversity in life comes from where we spend our time. And our time is spent at work, which is fortunate if you are living out what you see as your purpose and also fortunate if you're just working a job on the path to your purpose. Ultimately, *The Identity ATM* is meant to remind us that value in our day-to-day isn't always obvious. Perhaps it is something to be sought out.

When life is easy, values remain untested. It is simple to say that honesty matters until telling the truth comes with consequences. It is easy to say that perseverance is important until every option except quitting seems to have disappeared. Adversity forces a reckoning. It does not ask what we say we believe; it demands to know what we are willing to prove through action.

This process is uncomfortable. It requires letting go of the illusion that identity is built in moments of ease. Growth comes through conflict, resistance, and challenge. Values are refined when they are put under pressure. Our values remain hypothetical, possibly never even fully formed without hardship. Whatever background you come from on the spectrum of religious zealot to anti-anything spiritual, hardship exists for whatever reason, and it desires to control why you believe what you believe and how you are going to respond to it.

Banks as Boundaries

Boundaries protect identity just as banks protect money. Our values are shaped by influences like family, mentors, and experiences, forming the structure that guides us. Some boundaries strengthen us while others limit us. Examining and reinforcing the right ones ensures resilience, allowing identity to remain firm, even when adversity tests its foundation.

Resilience is what allows identity to be unshaken by circumstance. It 'insures' our bank accounts of self-esteem and confidence that our values are not overspent with external pressures but remain constant, giving us a sense of direction no matter what we face. In the end, identity and resilience are intertwined. One without the other is incomplete. Identity gives us purpose, but resilience ensures we do not lose that purpose when tested. The process of self-discovery is not about finding an easy path but about ensuring that when difficulty arises, we are prepared to remain true to ourselves. The question is not whether adversity will come—it will. The real question is whether we will allow it to break us or use it to refine and strengthen who we are. Those who build a strong identity and pair it with resilience will not only endure hardship but will emerge from it with greater clarity, strength, and purpose.

Questions for Reflection:

1. What adversity in your life makes it difficult to see your true identity?
2. What values do you believe define you, and have they ever been tested under adversity?
3. How have the "banks" in your life—family, mentors, culture, or experiences—shaped your values?
4. How much emotional equity is invested into your career or organization?
5. How do you process adversity to learn and grow from it?
6. In what ways have you demonstrated resilience in your life?

Conclusion: The Journey from Transactions to Transformation

Personal health, much like financial health, requires discipline. As we wrap up this book, please determine how this can be as practical as possible in maintaining discipline to access the Identity ATM. As you've noticed, this isn't a very static book. I intentionally stayed away from limiting this book to a long list of steps for you to do for your life to go exactly as you want it to. Life rarely turns out exactly how we think it will, which is exactly why we need to invest more in our thoughts. My hope is this is received as a self-investment book that requires a grasp of your context. Process the transactions that are taking place in your life, and more importantly, learn how the Identity ATM's expressions are transforming you as a result of them. The power to craft an identity lies within oneself, waiting to be funded.

The mental landscape we've journeyed across is deeply embedded within our psyche. Our emotions, thoughts, and experiences connect how we process our identity to how we express it. Through the chapters of this book, we've sought to understand, commit, and develop ourselves, especially in the mix of challenging emotions like guilt and shame. This primary transformative power of self-awareness is the first step toward change or growth. By drawing parallels between our identity and an ATM, we've emphasized how invaluable it is to invest in emotional and mental health and the corresponding connections to the physical and spiritual realms.

While guilt and shame are often perceived as negative emotions, this book has shown how they are value-added catalysts for profound rapport with our identity. Constructive guilt can teach responsibility and empathy while healing from shame can lead us on the path to mitigate risky behavior. Demystifying these emotions unearths their potential to be not labeled as withdrawals but unpretentious deposits to an established self.

Our exploration into one's context underscored the adage, "No man is an island." We are inevitably shaped by our surroundings, whom we bank with emotionally, such as family, friends, faith, and work. Recognizing this can equip us with the resilience to retain our definitive selves amidst external pressures. It teaches us the value of selective permeability – absorbing what edifies us and deflecting what doesn't align with our core. Additionally, the power of personal narratives is displayed in their ability to furnish innovative boundaries and remove barriers to growth. By being active authors of these narratives, we can craft tales of resilience, hope, and triumph.

The concept of emotional well-being, viewed as a balance sheet introduced in the latter part of our journey, underlines the essence of this entire exploration. Emotional wealth isn't just about moments of joy but about sustained well-being, a balance between our emotional assets and liabilities. While life will invariably present difficulties, making many withdrawals, our approach determines how much we have left after the emotional bills are paid.

While this book shares insights and tools, the real journey begins with you, the reader. You may be an individual on that journey to self-discovery or an organizational leader wanting to increase your talent management and professional development skills. You may be newly married and benefit from seeing the transactions in that bond with your spouse, which can make or break the bank of family. Perhaps you're a parent who has been engulfed with thoughts of failing your children, projecting or displacing your own shame onto them. Some of you are clergy leaders needing to get across to your respective community the importance of being funded by God's love, mercy, and forgiveness.

The ultimate dynamic here is realizing everyone's path is unique. The balance checks discussed here aid a thought-provoking life and emotional wealth. Regularly taking stock of your feelings, beliefs, and narratives amplifies the powerful tool of introspection. Seeking support, be it professional counseling, support groups, or trusted friends, opens our minds to clarify the banks relied upon. Never underestimate the healing power of shared experiences and guidance. You are challenging yourself and stepping out of your comfort zone to grow on the fringes of discomfort. Practicing compassion towards yourself and others focuses on the values you know will get you across the emotional landscape of your life. Journaling, creating art, or any other medium chronicling your journey can be therapeutic and offer insights into identity development.

Emotions can brighten or darken our world. Without them, our world would be monochromatic. This book has been an invitation to explore life's twists and turns and to emerge with a deeper appreciation for the richness of the human experience. Remember, again, the story doesn't end here. Your narrative is continually evolving, and with the insights and tools shared here for the journey, you're better equipped to craft a legacy of authentic emotional vibrancy. Embrace transactions that abide in your Identity ATM and thrive amidst life's experiences and expressions.

Look back at the picture at the beginning of this book. Not the cover, but the drawing of an ATM machine, connected to banks and simultaneously making transactions. Our lives are not much different. It would be naïve to suggest we are only connected to one bank or that we are only encountering one transaction at a time. Think back to the story in the beginning used to illustrate someone who accesses the Identity ATM on a regular basis. In the end, it helps you keep your priorities in check and is a platform to spring from if you choose to invest in yourself and others more.

Hopefully, I have expressed how amazing the Identity ATM is and its ability to make all of life's transactions happening at once not so overwhelming. Additionally, the Identity ATM is for couples who want to draw closer to one another, parents who are serious about building up their children, and leaders who simply want a methodology to caring for their employees. In the end though, we should also not be so naïve to think everyone's Identity ATM looks and operates the same. Like an ATM built this year compared to one from ten years ago, you may notice higher efficiency in speed, a friendlier user interface, and even a nicer design. After years of accessing and learning how to use the Identity ATM, you may find yourself to be that newer, faster model of a confident person in your home or work. You're no longer responding with accusations or excuses because you know that comes from depleted accounts of self-esteem. Consider the ways you'd like to become value added to the others around you, such as to your spouse, your kids, your coworkers. Let your Identity ATM provide you with enough currency of self-esteem and confidence to guide you through not just the transactions but the transformations that take place in life.